Princes of the
Working Valley

THE DAY & NIGHT BOOK OF
TWO DOLCOATH MINE CAPTAINS
1822–23

Allen Buckley

ISBN–10 **1 85022 209 6**
ISBN–13 **978 185022 209 5**

Published by Truran,
Croft Prince, Mount Hawke,
Truro, Cornwall TR4 8EE

www.truranbooks.co.uk

Truran is an imprint of Truran Books Ltd

Printed and bound in Cornwall by R. Booth Ltd,
Antron Hill, Mabe, Penryn, TR10 9HH

All spellings from the Day and Night Book are as the original

CONTENTS

Foreword 5

Introduction 7

The Dolcoath Mine Management, Technical Staff & Office 17

Responsibilities of Dolcoath 'Day & Night' Captains 27

Tin Mining at Dolcoath 44

Bal Maidens 48

Attitudes to Life, Materialism, Religion & Philosophy 60

The Captains' Use of the English Language 70

Neighbouring Mines 75

Bolenowe Mine 81

The Mine at Surface 86

Food & Drink 90

Conclusion 92

The Miners 96

The Bal Maidens 128

A Simple Glossary 131

Bibliography 134

Acknowledgements 135

In Memory of Clive Carter

Descended from generations of Dolcoath miners,
he was a man of many talents and great generosity.

FOREWORD

The history of the unique manuscript behind this book is as follows. An octavo notebook of some 200 pages, it survived for about a century in the Dolcoath Mine account-house at Camborne among thousands of ledgers, plans and records. In the late 1930s when the building was to became Dolcoath Technical School this vast archive was removed to a summerhouse at Lowenac, Camborne, and during the war had to be jettisoned to make way for a W.V.S. food store. However when Dolcoath Mine Ltd came to an end in the early 1920s certain items, notably with family connections, were removed by Captain R. Arthur Thomas, son of and successor to Captain Josiah Thomas (d.1901) and also a great-grandson of Captain James Thomas' brother Charles, to his home at Polstrong, Camborne. The 'Day and Night Captains' book passed to R.A. Thomas' son Captain A. Leonard Thomas, who did his best to sort out and list all these mining documents and letters going back to the late 18th century. In 1980, as security against the possible loss of a sole copy, I made photocopies of the manuscript (one for Cornwall Records Office at Truro, one for our own family archive) and also arranged for a typed transcript (in several copies). Before his death in October 1985, Leonard Thomas had given most of what he held to Camborne School of Mines, assuming (as it happens, incorrectly) that this would guarantee their safekeeping in Cornwall. In fact by 1994 the holding, catalogued in outline, had been removed to the library of the University of Exeter, where it was accessed as 'the Thomas Collection'. It remains to be seen whether this, and much else of a purely Cornish nature that in the last half-century has found its way to Exeter, will ever return to a future University of Cornwall.

This fascinating work, a continuous exchange of views and more factual information between the young William Petherick and the older James Thomas, has long deserved selective publication with a full commentary. Captain Jimmy Thomas, who as a lad attended John Wesley's last service at the Pit and whose father William Thomas indeed entertained John Wesley in his thatched farmhouse, has never been forgotten by his descendants; in my case, I write as the great-grandson of Captain Jimmy's great-nephew Josiah. When I (often) visit Bolenowe, our ancestral village, I always pause to see the old man's granite house and nice garden; in the past, too, to walk down the Brea stream valley to the much-changed ravine by Dolcoath, where the outflow from Crofty used to convert this stream into the Red River. What all the letters of the two men give us is not an 'official' record of a great mine. It is a picture of something far harder to evaluate today – life as it was, with its pastimes, prejudices, special vocabulary, and depiction of mining practices that one cannot always extract from less personal documents. How on earth, nearly two centuries afterwards, does one begin to edit and to explain everything penned by these two rather different characters? Very few of us could, today. Allen Buckley, in his joint capacities as practical miner and prolific historian, stands easily foremost as the man for the job. That he has taken it on and completed the task with such thoroughness and erudition must be a matter for rejoicing. For my own part it has been a pleasure to help, in a minor fashion, from the sidelines. Not since the late A.K. Hamilton Jenkin has anyone really managed to get inside the thoughts, private lives and off-duty moments of our mining forbears. This is a splendid piece of work, again, on Allen's part; and as the present head of the Camborne family once graced by Captain Jimmy – farmer, Methodist, mine agent, less-then-successful adventurer, a personal bridge between a late medieval and a relatively modern world – I want to record my gratitude, my relief that I abandoned the idea of editing the document myself(!), and my strongest recommendation to you all. Buy this book, and then make sure that you read it from cover to cover.

CHARLES THOMAS
November 2006

INTRODUCTION

For generations mine captains in Cornish mines left notes for their colleagues coming on shift or core. These notes, sometimes in notebooks and, undoubtedly, sometimes on slips of paper, informed the recipient of what had been done on the previous shift, what needed doing, what problems had occurred, what gear was required and anything else that the mine captain needed to know. Perhaps the earliest extant journal of this type is the one written by Captain James Thomas and Captain William Petherick between December 1822 and October 1823. This 'Day & Night Book' is the most informative account of how an early nineteenth century copper mine worked: what the relations between miner and management were like, what the responsibilities of mine captains were, how they interacted with the manager and the purser of the mine, what their attitude was to safety underground, how they treated the men under them and how the miners viewed them. The comments of these two remarkable mine captains also reveal their attitudes to religion, to superstition, to science and 'modern' philosophy and to their families and friends.

Their shared educational background and experience is also evident in their writings, and despite the difference in their ages, one was in his mid-forties and the other his mid-twenties, they were both taught to a similar standard in the village or 'dame' schools they attended. Some of these schools were properly endowed, usually by the Basset or Pendarves families, and had qualified school teachers. Camborne, Penponds and Redruth had such schools during the eighteenth and nineteenth centuries. Supplementing these well organised parish or village schools, were the informal institutions run by less-educated men and women. The poet John Harris, whose father and brother were both mentioned in the journal, attended schools of this latter type. His first school was run by Dame Trezone, who was remembered for her red hair and snuff-taking. He was then sent to a school at Troon Chapel run by Dame Penpraze and then to one run by a Mr Reed, a harsh and ferocious man, who beat the boys with a piece of wood with nails in it. The terrified boy begged his parents to send him somewhere else, and he eventually crossed the valley from Bolenowe to Forest Gate, where a one-legged ex-miner called Roberts taught him the three 'Rs'. Both mine captains were brought up with similar educational opportunities as Harris, and probably shared similar experiences.

William Petherick's 'dedication' at the beginning of the book sets the tone for the whole 201 page manuscript. It is headed and dated *Night 9th Dec'r 1822* and it provides the best introduction to their wonderful book:

Capt'n James:
It is customary when an author has finish'd the writing of a book in manuscript to compose a dedication fraught (in general) with the most egregious flattery to some great man or other, his patron, sometimes with & sometimes without his consent. Of course, a great task on this said patron, he is to recommend the work to ev'ry one to those who are not dependant on him, as well as to those who are, & in order the more effectually to complete the sale of the work (he) must have recourse to puffs of ev'ry description: all this trouble belongs to the patron, only of the tricks made use of by the author (him) we will here say nothing, but suppose we've a mind to. Now I think we may (be) different to all other authors & dedicate (our) book at its commencement & the great patron I would recommend shall be – Our Noble Selves. Knights of the most Honourable order of Beef Stews & Steaks. Knights Companions of the Roast Goose & Generals of the Morning Rashers & Princes of the Working Valley.

By this means we give no patron any trouble whatever, we shall not want to sell our manuscript & have no occasion whatever for puffs of any kind or denomination under the sun or moon. Its not ev'ry patron who can muster such a grand sett of titles & (altogether) so very honourable as those I have enumerated. Our only object will be to give each other as clear ideas on any subject which may concern us in as clear & explicit a manner as possible, not curtailing anything so as to leave any doubt of our intentions nor at the same time drawling out a slight subject with a tail like the tail of a comet, but let us stick to the old saying: 'I do not shite nor thick nor thin, but in the middling way'.

Its time to finish this dedication, both descriptive & sentimental, for I'm sure if this subject has not been drawn out like the tail of a comet, at least its drawn out like a lady's fart, that is to say its brought to a very fine point – there is nothing new tonight, I wish you could get a lantern from Capt Robin tomorrow for me, and there's no coal here. Wm Petherick.

This introduction by Captain William Petherick sets the mood, which prevails throughout most of the daily comments. It is light-hearted, irreverent and amusing, but set in the very serious context of a highly dangerous working environment. Right at the end of the dedication to the unique patrons, themselves, Petherick refers to the area of responsibility of these two men – *Princes of the Working Valley*. The Valley Section of Dolcoath stretched along the two branches of Main Lode from Gossan Shaft on the western side of the Red River valley to Water Whim (Valley/Eastern) Shaft on the eastern boundary of Dolcoath. These two branches were referred to at the time as North Valley and South Valley lodes, and sometimes North and South lodes. The section also included the workings at the north-eastern side of the mine between Roskear Broase and Wheal Susan, at Tuckingmill. Thus, this crescent shaped section included some of the widest workings on Main Lode and some of the less-important and narrower workings on North and South Entral Lodes, and Roskear Broase Lode, as well as the shallow workings at Wheal Susan.

The main body of the entries deal with the captain's daily or nightly round of visits underground and the discharge of responsibilities at surface, together with comments on the food available in their offices, and general gossip. Altogether the workload for these 'day and night' captains was formidable, especially when their other time-consuming activities are taken into account. James Thomas, for example, not only farmed a small-holding at Bolenowe, two miles south of Dolcoath, to and from which he walked daily, but he also managed a small mine there called variously, 'Bolenowe, South Bolenowe' or 'Wheal Butterfly'. William Petherick had an important interest in West Wheal Wellington Mine, at Camborne. Both Thomas and Petherick were also constantly called upon to 'dial', i.e. survey, several neighbouring mines in the district, travel long distances on horse back to evaluate mining gear being sold, or inspect mines for the agents. Added to the above, they also led busy social lives, went to chapel regularly, and not just for Sunday service, for they also attended lectures by itinerant or local preachers. Some of their most interesting entries deal with such theological lectures and debates. The journal probably represents one of the most revealing pieces of literature produced by working-class men of the early nineteenth century, its unselfconscious nature making the insight into their characters all the more fascinating and their naïve and disingenuous comments refreshingly honest and believable.

We cannot know how typical these two men were of their time. Their entries in the journal and references to their many acquaintances indicate that the attitudes they displayed were not unusual. Their interest in religion was certainly shared by many contemporaries and there is sufficient evidence of widespread attendance at religious meetings and revivals to indicate a general concern for spiritual things. Likewise, their love of the visiting fair, delight in the sight of attractive women, enjoyment of a good joke or an entertaining book, may not have been typical although the evidence suggests that it was certainly not unusual.

Captain James Thomas (1778–1867)
James Thomas was born at Bolenowe, in the south-east corner of Camborne Parish, and baptised in the parish church on 25 April 1778. His father was William Thomas of Bolenowe, whose family had moved from Gulval to the Bolenowe district at the end of the seventeenth century. For generations the family had been farmers and churchwardens at Gulval, and when they moved to the Illogan-Camborne area they added tin streaming and mining to their occupations. Demographic movement of this type was fairly typical of the time, as the expanding mining industry of the Camborne-Illogan district drew workers into the district from agricultural areas of Cornwall. On 22 August 1798 James married Jenefer Penpraze of Crowan at the parish church there. Like his older brother, Charles, James followed his father into mining, and like Charles he went to Cooks Kitchen Mine as a copper miner. James was born in the thatched cottage built at Bolenowe by his grandfather, Jacob, and in 1801/2 inherited his father's lease of several acres of rough farmland, whilst his older brother, Charles, gained the family property at 'Nagoby' (Knavegoby), near Beacon. His oldest brother, William, also farmed land at Bolenowe, that their father had previously leased. James built his own two-storey house at Bolenowe, which was complete by about 1820. The house is still there.

James and Jenefer (Jane) Thomas had seven children, two of whom died young, one on his first day and the other when she was six years old. His four surviving sons all became mine agents or captains, and three of them, William, Henry and Charles, migrated to Ireland as the mines there were opened up. They all three died there, although as was usual among the migrating miners and engineers from Cornwall, they kept in contact with their families at home, and James visited them in Ireland in 1843, when he was about 65 years old. His oldest son, James, born in 1800, married his cousin, Eleanor Penpraze, became a mine agent at Camborne Vean Mine by 1828, retired early to Bolenowe, due to bad health, and died there in 1851.

James Thomas was a devout and well-known Wesleyan local preacher, as was his father, William, who once entertained John Wesley in his house at Bolenowe. When James was eleven years old, he walked from Bolenowe to Gwennap Pit, to listen to the last sermon John Wesley preached there, on Sunday August 23 1789. He remained faithful to the Wesleyans for the rest of his life, and he influenced many who became better known than him. The young John Harris, the 'miner poet', who was born and brought up at Six Chimneys, above Bolenowe village, spoke fondly of 'Capt Jemmy Thomas', who 'threw open his library door to me'. He loaned him books and encouraged him in his studies, both sacred and profane. James had a well-stocked library, which he made available to all those who would benefit, and the poet certainly took advantage. Mark Harris, a Wesleyan preacher who wrote an account of his own life and times, referred to James Thomas several times. He spoke of meeting the old mine captain, 'aged, decrepit and grey', in 1848, when he was about seven or eight years old, and James Thomas was about seventy. Harris mentioned Thomas' walk to Gwennap Pit when he was eleven years old, that he had joined Troon 'class meeting' when he was eighteen years old, and had been joined by his brothers and sisters in the Society. Thomas had told Harris how Troon got its own chapel in 1795 and that when he was about eighteen months in the Society, he had his own Bible class at Dower, about two miles south of Troon, now Lower Carwynnen. From the age of 22 James Thomas had been a Wesleyan local preacher, with his own classes at Treslothan and Dower. Captain Thomas was undoubtedly deeply religious, with a profound and sincere devotion to his Lord and his religion, but he was also a man of his class and his time. His religiousness did not make him self-righteous or po-faced and there was nothing smug or self-satisfied about him. When called for his language was as rich and pithy as any other miner, and when needed he was capable of vulgar humour, which a later generation of Wesleyans might have found distasteful. His sense of humour and language were basic, and his view of life and his fellow sinners earthy and realistic, and he tended to express himself accordingly.

James Thomas was a Freemason. On August 8 1823 he wrote: *I want to be home tomorrow as it's a grand sitting. I suppose a plenty of Masons will be there. Please to run up here for me.* It appears to be the only reference to Freemasons in the journal, and as Thomas wanted the day off to attend the *grand sitting*, it seems to have been a special occasion. There is no record of a Masonic lodge at Camborne as early as 1823, so unless the movement had a branch earlier than hitherto thought, he probably attended at Druid's Lodge, which met at Fosses Hotel, Redruth. Thomas' Masonic membership warns us against generalisations, for although it is widely held that Methodism condemned Freemasonry, it apparently did not inhibit this devout and widely-respected Wesleyan preacher from being a member. Given the predominance of Methodism among Cornish miners going abroad, it is of interest that their networking patterns included membership of Masonic lodges in Australia and America, along with the 'Cousin Jack' network and attendance at the local chapels in the frontier towns to which the miners went.

James began his career as a junior mine captain at Cooks Kitchen in 1797, when he was only 19 years old. When Dolcoath re-opened he moved there, and he appears to have been a 'day & night' captain there from about 1815, when he was in his upper-thirties. These 'inferior' mine captains were almost always experienced miners who occupied the front-line of mine management. They dealt with the day to day running of the mine underground, where they settled disputes, negotiated special payments and ensured the work was done properly and safely, and also had various responsibilities at surface. Captain Thomas was mainly responsible for re-opening Bolenowe Mine, from about 1822, and during the following year he spent a considerable amount of time supervising the draining, clearing and securing of the old workings, before negotiating with his fellow mine captains at various mines in Camborne for appropriate machinery. He managed to involve other mining men, miners, mine captains and investors in the project, and he suffered at times from the sarcasm of Captain Petherick on the size and importance of the mine. The Day & Night Book reveals Captain Thomas to have been a vigorous and energetic man, who undertook a prodigious work-load and then walked over two miles home to Bolenowe to lift his potatoes, carry his hay or cut his furze.

Captain William Petherick (1796–1844)

William Petherick was born in the year 1796, the son of Ezekiel Petherick of Phillack. We know far less about William's background, than we do about that of his colleague James Thomas, but we do know a considerable amount about his activities at Dolcoath, where he rose to become mine manager. His father, Ezekiel, was born in 1764 and died in 1848, and so he was in his early thirties when William was born, and when William died prematurely at the age of 47, in January 1844, his 80 year old father was still alive, dying in 1848 at the age of 84 years. We do not know if Petherick ever married, although when the Day & Night Book was written, he was living in Camborne with his parents, and at least one entry suggests that he maintained contact with his family's parish of origin, Phillack. It is believed that he lived in a property owned by his uncle, Captain John Rule, at Camborne, close to the present railway station. By the time of the Tithe Apportionment Map, 1840, William was living at Camborne Churchtown. Puns by Captain James Thomas on the name *Patience* and possibly the surname *Wills* might indicate that in 1823, he was interested in, if not actually courting a young lady of that name.

Although six years older than William West, the famous engineer of Fowey Consols, Petherick was brought up close to West's home at Dolcoath Farm, and it is possible they were friends and attended the same school. Betty Michell ran a sort of Dame school at Dolcoath to which West was sent, and it is possible that Petherick was also a pupil there. Like Trevithick, a generation earlier, the boys did not learn much and spent their time sky-larking and generally amusing themselves. Betty Michell was known to the boys as 'Old Betty Hip' on account of her being lame and walking with a severe limp. She taught them the rudiments of reading, writing and summing, but her main preoccupation was her supply of gin, which the boys were sent for regularly.

Petherick was the nephew of Captain John Rule, manager of Dolcoath between 1806 and 1834, his mother, Elizabeth, being Rule's younger sister. He was appointed 'day & night' captain in May 1822, when he was about 25 years old, and he worked in the Valley Section of Dolcoath Mine on the opposite shift to Captain James Thomas. His lively, and often irreverent entries in the journal show he was a young man with a wicked sense of humour, who did not suffer fools gladly, but frequently displayed a sympathetic understanding of the problems of the poor miners. He was wittily sarcastic about the older man's superstitious confidence in the existence of a miner's 'dream lode', and he gave a very amusing description of a visiting preacher's incompetent sermon, but he could wax philosophical, sentimental and even spiritual, when reflecting upon the birth of Christ, 1,822 years earlier. *The most prominent feature which strikes the imagination is the birth of a Saviour who took the form of a man upon him having the great & noble object in view, the redemption of the whole human race.*

William Petherick was a man who felt deeply about his responsibilities, who was honest and expected the workforce to be likewise. He had no sympathy for malingerers, those who attempted fiddles, and bal maidens who stole from the mine could expect no mercy from him. He expected miners to keep to their agreements, with the management and with each other. As well as having a close friendship with James Thomas, twenty years older than him, he got on well with his cousins, some of whom also worked at the mine, and in particular with his cousin, Captain John Rule junior. Together these two intelligent young men showed an interest in such things as improved ventilation, studying the air-flow between shafts and winzes, and checking temperatures throughout their sections. They were enthusiastic supporters of the various scientists who visited the mine in the 1820s, to study geology, ventilation and better mining practice. When John Rule junior left the mine to work for John Taylor, the principal adventurer at Gwennap Consols and United Mines, Petherick replaced him as the manager's right-hand man, and when Captain Rule was 79 years old, and no longer able to shoulder all the responsibility of running the great mine, William became joint manager with his uncle, and supported him until Rule's death in 1834. Thereafter, William Petherick became sole manager of Dolcoath, and for the ten years he held that position, he displayed a strength of character and resilience unsurpassed in the history of the mine. He held the whole operation together and kept the mine going when all around him: adventurers, mine pundits and consultant mine agents, shook their heads and predicted disaster. Supported by Captain Charles Thomas, who was in turn to replace him as manager, Petherick brought in improvements and economies, and even persuaded the adventurers to spend money on improving the working conditions of the miners themselves: better changing facilities and hot soup for miners when they returned to surface, were just two of the innovative changes he brought to the mine.

Outside the mine Petherick was seen as a go ahead and intelligent mine manager, who also acted as managing agent for other mines, such as East Pool, in 1834. He appears to have also been associated with East Wheal Crofty, and one of their shafts was named after him. Articles in the *Transactions of the Royal Geological Society of Cornwall* quote him on the crosscourses and lode structures of Dolcoath and the geology of neighbouring mines, the 1843 volume referring to him as "Captain Petherick, the intelligent manager of Dolcoath". The *West Briton* of November 27 1835 contains letters from John Budge, a respected engineer and Petherick, disputing points about steam engines with James Sims, another noted Cornish steam engineer. Petherick's interest in steam engines was apparently quite deep, and he was associated with William West, chief engineer at Fowey Consols, over the erection of one of the best performing Cornish engines of the period. This 80 inch engine was the subject of a trial to test its performance, and it is of interest that the names of the referees included John Budge, James Thomas and Thomas Petherick. Budge was the Camborne engineer Petherick was associated with in his letters to James Sims, it is probable that Thomas Petherick was a relative and James Thomas was probably his old colleague and friend from Dolcoath.

Valley Section of Dolcoath Mine
The principal purpose of the Day & Night Book was to inform the captain coming on shift what had happened on the previous shift and what needed doing on the next. With this in mind it is hardly surprising that the bulk of the journal is concerned with the day to day running of *the Valley*, an important section of one of the world's greatest copper mines. During the ten months that the journal covers, from December 9 1822 to October 16

1823, Thomas and Petherick regularly visited and inspected the ends and pitches on nineteen different levels, from Shallow Adit down to the 200fm level, although the two deepest levels visited by Captain James Thomas on January 9 1823, the 190 and 200fm levels, lay outside their bailiwick, in Middle Section, where Captain Tregoning and another captain were in charge. Valley Section's deepest level was the 145fm level, which joined this easterly section to the Middle or Bullen Garden Section. Most of the tribute pitches in the Valley were below the 40fm level and apart from winzes between levels for improved ventilation and exploration, no sinking took place during the period of the Day & Night Book. In fact, the mine was not deepened from the early 1820s until Captain Charles Thomas began to sink below the 210fm level in 1849.

The two mine captains were responsible for the maintenance and efficient use of all the shafts in their section. These included Gossan Shaft, on the western side of the Red River Valley, which marked their western boundary, and Water Whim Shaft, also known as Valley or Eastern Shaft, which marked their eastern boundary with Cooks Kitchen. Two other important shafts were North Valley or Valley Shaft and South Valley Shaft. Machine Shaft, Roskear Broase Shaft, Entral Shaft, Water Stile Shaft, East Valley Shaft, Martins Shaft and Wheal Susan Shaft were also under their jurisdiction.

The journal refers to several mineralised structures or lodes exploited in the Valley and its adjacent workings. Main Lode, east of Gossan Shaft usually referred to as North Valley or South Valley Lode, was worked in very wide stopes. Timber stull pieces purchased at Perran in August were said to be *not less than 20 feet in length*. North Entral, South Entral and Roskear Broaze lodes were worked, as well as a lode called Roskear Broaze South Lode (*R.B.s.Lode*). Another lode, which had the intriguing name of *Roarer Lode*, was also worked for tin and copper.

THE DOLCOATH MINE MANAGEMENT, TECHNICAL STAFF & OFFICE

In 1808 the Reverend Richard Warren visited Dolcoath and described the mine management as being comprised of purser or bookkeeper, 'chief captain or manager' and eight 'inferior' captains, those acting under the authority of the manager. There was also an engineer. Whether these eight captains were all underground captains or included the surface or 'grass' captains, he does not say. The 1822–23 journal refers to some thirteen mine captains, as well as the purser and the mine manager. However, it is not always clear what the responsibilities of those individual men were, and at least three of them were employed by neighbouring mines.

At the top of the tree was the mine purser. He was referred to in the journal in connection with discipline, with authority to erect a new building for the night shift mine captain to use, and as a final arbiter in disputes. The first reference was on May 21, when the manager demanded to know why captains Petherick and Thomas were failing to stay all night, when working at surface. *Capt Rule has been talking to me again about our not staying here all night. I told him to build a new house for us & he might depend on our staying, otherwise he would get neither of us to stay here all night at all. He says we ought to have a new house & he will talk with Mr Reynolds about it.* Mr Reynolds, the Dolcoath purser, was William Reynolds of Trevenson House, Pool, and he was also the agent for Sir Francis Basset, Lord de Dunstanville. Not only did he hold the purse strings, but he was also needed to make decisions on such things as new buildings, even when, as in this case, it was probably no more than a wooden hut. Reynolds was also the final 'court of appeal' when miners were dissatisfied with the decisions of the captains and the manager. On September 8 Petherick related the story of *Old Tom Crase*, who demanded to know why Petherick had not sent his son work with *Oppy & pare*. Crase swore that if he got no satisfaction *he would go to Capt Rule &*

from thence to Mr Reynolds & he would see whether he couldn't get employ for his son or not. I told him he had better go to Mr Reynolds at once as 'twould save him the labour of seeing Capt Rule. He went of in great rage I believe swearing. A more common activity for the purser had to do with deciding on action to be taken in difficult cases of discipline. On April 10 Captain Thomas called on the manager to discuss such a case, and reported that it would be taken to Mr Reynolds that weekend. Until the purser had heard the evidence the miners, Rogers & ptrs, were to cease working. Petherick replied that Reynolds would be at the mine on the Saturday and he would be on hand to give evidence. On September 3 the same miners were again in trouble, and once again Reynolds was involved. *Peter Grangey & Rogers & all the whole tote of them were all turned off today by Mr Reynolds for a sett of rogues & vagabonds & the pitch sett anew for 6s/10d.*

After the mine purser came the mine manager or senior captain. From 1806 until 1834 this position was held by Captain John Rule (1751–1834). Captain Rule was referred to throughout the Day & Night Book, and he made all final decisions on important changes in practice, granting of pitches or contracts, and on new developments. Although most day-to-day decisions were left to his captains, the manager had the authority to over-rule them. He frequently ordered the two 'day & night' captains to go to other mines to dial and measure the workings, evaluate and purchase materials for sale, and check current tin prices at various smelting houses and negotiate its sale. In matters of mining Captain Rule was supreme. If he had gained his position in part due to being part of a close-knit group of Camborne mining men, he was, nevertheless, an experienced mine captain and more than capable of running the great mine. He continued the practice of showing favour to his relatives, for his senior captain was his oldest son, John junior, other sons were also captains at Dolcoath, and Captain Petherick, who was to succeed him, was his nephew, the son of his sister. During Rule's tenure Dolcoath regained the position it had held in the 1760s and 70s, of being the greatest copper mine in Cornwall and the rest of the world. Unfortunately, its success in mining out its once-vast copper reserves, led to its decline as a copper mine, and Rule's last years saw a constant struggle against diminishing returns and increasing costs.

Captain John Rule was highly regarded by his contemporaries as a first-class mine manager. He was respected by his captains and his miners, and his sense of humour and fairness made him popular also. He was 72 years old when he set up and participated in a joke he played on his two 'grass captains' at Truro. He got the younger captains to set up captains Robin and Jilbert, by making them pay for wine they had no money for, and then getting an old coal woman to follow them around Truro to embarrass them. Petherick commented: *Capt Rule is enjoying the thought of your swigging (Glossary) Capts Jilbert & Robin, he says he hopes you'll do for them.* It is easy to understand why he was so highly thought of by his men. The journal makes it apparent that he ruled with a light touch and not as a disciplinarian. By the time he gave up sole management of Dolcoath, and made his nephew, William Petherick, his joint manager, he was 79 years old, although he remained ostensibly at the helm until he was 83.

Among the mine captains was the manager's right-hand man, his eldest son, John Rule junior. He was referred to several times in the Day & Night Book, and he was usually exercising authority and making decisions either in conjunction with his father or in his own name. He was a close friend of William Petherick, his cousin, and they worked together in assisting scientists and others investigate aspects of mine ventilation and working practice. By 1824 Rule had joined John Taylor's Consols and United Mines at Gwennap, and by 1825 he had been sent to Pechuca, Mexico, where he managed the great Real del Monte Mines for Taylor. His fame in the new world possibly exceeded that attained by his contemporaries at home in Cornwall, and he became known as the Silver King of Mexico. His family erected memorials to the Cornish presence in Pechuca, including a clock tower with chimes like Big Ben. He founded a mining dynasty there and established one of the most enduring migration routes between the old and new worlds.

Another relative, who was probably another son of the manager, was Captain William Rule. There were two mentions of William in the journal, one, when he went with William Petherick to a smelting house to get a price for tin, and the other, when he joined Petherick in an inspection of James Thomas' Bolenowe Mine. Captain Charles Thomas, the older brother of James, was also a mine captain at Dolcoath, and he was mentioned in the journal on July 21 and August 18 1823. The entries show him discharging various responsibilities, including inspecting timberwork.

The entry of August 27 speaks of him going to Perran to purchase timber, perhaps for the place he had inspected on the 18ᵗʰ. Captain Tregoning was a 'day & night' captain for the Middle Section of the mine, the area comprising Bullen Garden workings. He was mentioned twice in the journal, once when he took Captain James Thomas to see the newly discovered tin lode on the 190 and 200fm levels, on January 9 1823, and the other time when Thomas asked Petherick to visit Bolenowe Mine and bring Captain Tregoning with him. Some years later, probably after 1834, when Dolcoath was in decline and laying men off, Captain Tregoning seems to have gone to East Wheal Crofty as a mine captain, for in that year a Captain Hugh Tregoning appears there, and with him was Captain John Lean, another former Dolcoath man. This Captain Lean was mentioned once in the journal, in association with Captain Jilbert, but whether he was a 'grass' captain or not, we cannot be certain.

Captains Christopher (Kit) Robin and Jilbert appear to have been surface or 'grass' captains, and their responsibilities were frequently concerned with sorting and weighing parcels of copper and tin ore. Robin and Jilbert were not particularly good at this aspect of their work, and they were in constant trouble with the samplers and the bal maidens. It is probable that they were former 'day & night' captains who were no longer fit to go underground and hence were given surface jobs. These two captains were constantly the butt of jokes and sarcastic comments on their ability to accurately sort and weigh ore. On December 18 1822 Petherick said: *I understand notwith- standing all the to do with Captain Robin & Captain Jilbert, had I been in Captain Rule's place neither of the two should weigh ore any more they make more noise than all the rest of the agents in the mine.* Petherick commented on January 2 that he had to obtain cost figures from Captain Robin *by main force,* and on February 20 he referred to Robin as so confused by the ore weighing process that he looked like he *been eaten & shitten again.* In June he commented again about Robin's lack of skill in weighing and sampling ores: *I thought the samplers would have refused to sample the 34 (tons), but Capt Kit Robin was in an uncommonly good temper for a wonder ... Capt Robin wished to take up the samples today, but I would not let him. He had a brave noise today about the tin, but he takes it all very easy & careless. Would it not be good if we were to put a little Cayenne Pepper in the hole of his (arse)?* Even the religious Captain Thomas joined in the joke, and exhorted

Petherick *don't forget the Cayenne Pepper for Capt Robin.* In July, Mr Bawden, a sampler for one of the copper companies, *said he had never weighed ore with Capt Robin, nor never would.* In August Petherick said: *Capt Robin is looking as blue as a yellow butterfly on account of the tin samples being sent to him numbered and ticketed like the (copper) ore samples,* and on September 4 after weighing some of the copper ore, Petherick arrived and sent the unfortunate Robin home.

It is hard not to feel sympathy for those two old mine captains, out of their depth and subject to being wound up and sometime even abused by their younger colleagues, but it was a mine, full of rough and ready men and women, and they themselves had been born and brought up in that atmosphere. For these two 'grass' captains, things were about to get even worse. On the night of September 22 Captain Thomas left a message for Captain Petherick in which he said he was to go to Truro in behalf of the mine, and that as Captain Robin was also going, he wondered if Petherick could ask him for a lift. Back came the reply that Robin and Jilbert were indeed going, by gig, and although they had not refused to take Thomas, they were clearly not keen to do so. Petherick then commented: *Be sure to give a good look out & see where they go to dinner.* Somewhat miffed, Thomas said *I suppose I can find the way without them,* and said he was determined to see where they dined. On the 24ᵗʰ Petherick explained the plot being hatched to embarrass the two older captains. *Capt Rule wishes you & Capt Harry to get Caps Jilbert & Robin to spend more money than they will receive. Go to dinner with them if possible & order 2 or 3 bottles of wine & make them pay their part & if Capt Harry can find any old coal woman with her cowal (Glossary) to dog them around the streets 'twould be glorious fun, for I think we shall want something or other to keep our spirits up on Saturday next, from what I can see of it.* Petherick added a footnote to the journal, in which the manager expressed his pleasure at the *swigging* of the two unfortunates. We can imagine these two working class men, who had made it in their world, dressed in their Sunday best to represent the most important mine in Cornwall to the debenture holders, being first embarrassed whilst dining among the well-off Truronian middle classes, and then being followed around the streets of Truro by a blackened old woman with a sack of coal on her back. They must have been mortified.

The above is the only reference to Captain Harry, but he does appear to have been a Dolcoath man, although what his specific job was we do not know. Three other mine captains are referred to in the journal, but it does not appear that they worked at Dolcoath. A Captain Skinner was mentioned in connection with West Wheal Wellington Mine, where Captain Petherick was an adventurer, and on July 30 1823 he accompanied Petherick when he inspected Bolenowe Mine.

Two other mine captains mentioned were captains Tucker senior and junior. Captain Tucker senior was an irascible old miner, who had a hot temper and was given to extremely violent and sometime obscene language. He worked at Wheal Francis, which lay on the western side of Camborne Vean Mine, near to Camborne Veor Farm. The first reference to him was on February 21 when Petherick visited him at Wheal Francis to discuss a problem that had arisen due to bad feeling over a dispute between miners over some tin. Thomas, Petherick and Tucker were determined to sort the problem out. On May 9 Petherick was again at Wheal Francis to see Captain Tucker, and this time Tucker showed no restraint in his reaction to what had happened. *I've been down to Wh. Francis today. Told the old Tucker about the business we were talking of last night. His words were, 'Some damned infernal bugger or other must have told them of it, who deserved to have his mouth stuffed with turd a fortnight old & condemned afterwards to have the pox to such a degree as for his limbs to drop off one by one.'* The final mention of the bad-tempered old man was July 23, when Petherick visited him and announced to Thomas that; *I've been to the old Capt Tucker's drinking tea this afternoon. What do you think of that???* Presumably, non-alcoholic tea was not the normal liquid imbibed by Captain Tucker and his guests.

Captain Tucker junior may well have been the son of the Wheal Francis mine captain, and the mine he appears to have been associated with was Camborne Vean Mine, next door to Wheal Francis. Like the older man young Tucker was credited with the telling of good stories, and on May 29 1823, when Petherick attended Camborne Vean survey day, he told Thomas he was to get his own back on him. *Tomorrow is Camborne Vean survey day & before dinner I shall give the young Tucker his due, 'tis what I've been aching for this long time.*

In 1822–23 Dolcoath had two engineers, Richard Jeffree (Jeffery) and James Gribble. Jeffree was the older man, being born in 1773, and he had been an assistant to Richard Trevithick when the great engineer had looked after Dolcoath's engines and invented the world's first locomotive, the 'Camborne Road Loco'. He had learned on-the-job, like so many of his contemporaries. Once Trevithick had moved almost permanently to London, and elsewhere, Jeffree had taken over as resident engineer at Dolcoath. Following criticism of the mine's engines, by Captain Joel Lean in his Reporter of 1812, Dolcoath made various changes, and one of them was to promote the 26 year old James Gribble from engineman at Wheal Gons and Stray Park to being joint-engineer with Jeffree. Gribble had also learned his trade though practical experience rather than formal training, and he was to be acknowledged as a brilliant and innovative engineer, by men such as Arthur Woolf, one of the greatest engineers of his day. Gribble has been credited with designing the 'Great' 76 inch engine erected at New Sump Shaft in 1816. Unfortunately, James Gribble died whilst still relatively young, at the age of 39, in April 1825. A young assistant to these joint engineers at Dolcoath was John West, the older brother to the more famous William West. He was employed at the mine in the early nineteenth century, and as his skill grew he became engineer to several important local mines, including Tincroft, East Pool, South Roskear and Wheal Providence. West does not appear in the journal.

Richard Jeffree appears only once in the Day & Night Book, but there are several references to James Gribble. In the entry for the night of August 26 1823 James Thomas tells Petherick he would not be in very early the next evening, *as Mr Jeffry was asking me to go to Wheal Neptune.* Thomas went on the 27th to look at the gear and machinery, which was for sale, but there was *Nothing at Wheal Neptune worth our notice … I am weary & tired riding & walking.* James Gribble's advice was sought by Captain Thomas over appropriate machinery for Bolenowe Mine, and on July 14 1823 Petherick commented: *Capt Rule was saying to me today that he thought James Gribble, engineer, would approve of that cylinder at Roskear Broase for Bolenowe.* Thomas responded by saying he would call down and see Gribble about it, and on the 16th Petherick talked of another prospective engine for Bolenowe: *How much does Mr Williams ask for his engine. Will it come cheaper than Jemmy Gribble's?* That night Thomas wrote: *I am going with Mr Gribble* to see Mr Williams's engine. *We shall see wether it is compleat & good or not and know the price, etc. If we can have a little engine second hand cheap, it will be exactly the thing we want.* On July 21 Thomas wrote: *I have been with Mr Gribble today, examining Roskear Broase cylinder, etc, with the nozells at Wheal Bryant, etc, I spoke to Capt Rule about them and he says that we shall have them in a moderate price, so I told him I would take them, as Capt Joe (Vivian) from South Roskear was waiting to accept if I refused. I think we shall get an engine cheap in this way.* Captain Thomas wasted no time in getting the Roskear Broase engine's cylinder, for three days later Petherick commented that Thomas had been too busy as he *heav'd* out the cylinder to write a report in the journal. It is interesting how 'day & night' captains were used to check out engines and other mining gear, and how the mine's engineers were ready with technical advice on machinery for other mines than Dolcoath.

A very important and highly thought of employee of Dolcoath was the assayer, John Phillips. He combined assaying with other office duties, such as bookkeeping. John Phillip's advice was constantly sought by the mine captains, for he not only acted as assayer at Dolcoath, but he was also a skilled surveyor and draughtsman. He was employed by East Wheal Crofty as surveyor and ran a night school for young miners. This school, called Camborne Mining School, was situated at Tuckingmill, and Phillips advertised it in the *Journal of the Royal Cornwall Polytechnic Society* (1839–41) along with his various inventions, like a 'portable trigonometer'. The 1842 government sponsored report on the Employment of Children, described Phillip's school. It was a day and evening school and sons of miners and young miners were taught there. Apart from reading and writing they were also instructed in the use of various mechanical contrivances found in mines, as well as being taught physics, chemistry, arithmetic and mensuration, which included the skills needed for accurate surveying. There were forty boys in the day school and twelve in the evening classes. The fees were £2–£3 a year. The school was approved by the Polytechnic Society. It was in such establishments that mine captains like James Thomas and William Petherick had learned the skills of dialling and surveying.

The journal refers to Phillips in his capacity of bookkeeper on several occasions, and typical entries are: *Please send up the Tribute Subsist book to John Phillips.* (Feb 27 1823) and: *I have weighed off the two parcels of ore today* with Mr Morcom ... *please to give John Phillips the account of it that he may put it in the book.* On September 17 1823 Captain Petherick speaks of Phillips as one of the adventurers in Bolenowe Mine, and jokingly says that if the mine has *cut rich, J Phillips, Richard Rule & myself are going to Scilly, Dublin, Paris, Cadiz, Pisa and the Isle of Scio, and where also I don't know as yet.* His role as the mine assayer was referred to on September 24, when Captain Thomas wrote to Captain Petherick: *I wish you would desire John Phillips to assay the stuff you see on the desk, and see if there is any copper in it – beg him to do it this day, as it came from Bolenowe, not from the + cut south, but from Engine Shaft. What to make of it I don't know ... if there is any copper in it, it will be worth something.* Petherick replied the next day: *The stone you left on the desk , J Phillips could not assay, but it was the general opinion of the men & Capt Rule amongst them, that there was no copper in it.* Undoubtedly, as Phillips and Petherick were adventurers in Bolenowe Mine, they would also have been disappointed with the lack of copper in the sample. On July 4 1823 Captain Thomas told Petherick of an appointment with Mr Pendarves, Bolenowe mineral lord, to arrange a meeting of Bolenowe adventurers. On the 16th he wrote: *The resolution signed at the meeting was to collect £5 per share – but I shall colect only 50/- from all those that I colected of last time. If you will be so good as to speak to Messers Joseph & William Rule to that affect, and if I could have the money on Saturday, I shall feel obliged. Try to see Mr Phillips too. I have spoken to Charles. I must try to get the money to pay the men on Saturday afternoon.* James Thomas had successfully involved an impressive group of Dolcoath men in his Bolenowe project, including those members of the Rule family, other mine captains including Petherick, and the mine assayer, John Phillips.

Outsiders who were regular visitors to Dolcoath were the agents of the copper smelting houses. Four were mentioned as frequently sampling ore at the mine: Messers Noel, Provis, Morcom and Bawden. Their names occur on numerous occasions, sorting, marking, weighing and sampling the parcels of copper ore. The bal maidens sometimes gave these outsiders a hard time, and there appears to have been much light-hearted banter between them. However, these samplers had as much trouble with captains Robin and Jilbert as from the bal maidens. As noted above, Mr Morcom plainly objected to working with the former. Sometimes the problems they encountered were not with the maidens or the incompetent captains, but with each other. Captain Petherick wrote in the journal of the night of February 21 1823: *There has been a dreadfull falling out between the samplers, poor buggers, let them get pleased again as soon as they think proper.* John Phillips, the assayer, kept the account book for the ore sampling.

RESPONSIBILITIES OF DOLCOATH 'DAY & NIGHT' CAPTAINS

A fascinating aspect of the Day & Night Book is what it tells us of how these mine captains worked and what their responsibilities were. Their principal area of concern was underground, with the miners, and so development and production were at the centre of most of their activity. Although they were involved with the setting of tribute pitches, the prime responsibility for this two-monthly auction lay with the mine manager, who undoubtedly delegated some of it to the senior captain in each section. Despite James Thomas' age, he was some twenty years older than William Petherick, it is not clear who was the senior man in the Valley Section, because although Thomas had the experience, Petherick was without a doubt the rising star and was highly thought of by his uncle, the manager John Rule. The journal makes many references to Petherick and Thomas renegotiating tribute agreements, varying details and making extra, unscheduled payments for unforeseen work. Stems, or 'day pay' was used as well as one-off cash payments. Miners who wished to abandon an unprofitable pitch or take on extra men or work their pitch (or pitches) differently, negotiated with the 'day & night' captain. Contravention of the original agreement, on the pitch limits or on aspects of working safely, were dealt with initially by these captains.

Development & Production

The daily task of the 'day & night' captain was to inspect the working places of the miners in his section. The three principal areas of these inspections were the tribute pitches, the development ends and the shafts. The first had to do primarily with production: to ensure that the tributers were working efficiently in breaking sufficient payable copper or tin ore in the stopes. The captain also had to keep a wary eye open for miners who, especially toward the end of a contract period, might salt away or disguise good grade ore, so that on setting or survey day he could get a better price for the pitch. He might also ensure that miners were not sharing out good ore with their mates on adjacent pitches for the same purpose. Tributers with more than one pitch might try to work them to their own advantage, especially where one contained good copper ore and the other tin. An interesting case was discussed by Captain Petherick in his note to Captain Thomas on the night of May 12 1823.

Captn James:
While I think of it & have a little time on hand, it may not be amiss to give you my thoughts respecting T Roberts & ptrs. You know they have two pitches amongst them, one copper the other tin. At certain times I know they have all been working the copper pitch while the tin pitch has been left idle & vice versa. Now, I do not think that this is as it should be. They should, in my opinion, confine themselves either to the one or the other, because it's waiting for any advantage which may arise in either pitch. Consequently, the other will be immediately deserted. Should it so happen, as the above supposed, all the blame will fall upon us. They will of course always work the best pitch leaving us to scramble out of any dilemma into which we may get by allowing them so great a latitude, directly contrary to the Rules of the Mine & to the discouragement of all our tributers, who ought to have as much privilege & encouragement as T Roberts & pare, for anything that I can see.
Wm Petherick

Captain Thomas was confident that he could *soon settle the business with them about having two pitches*, and said he would go down on May 14 for this purpose, but three months later, Tom Roberts and his pare had still not given up their determination to work these two pitches to their advantage rather than the mine's. On August 8 Roberts and his mates approached Thomas and asked him *to speak to Capt Rule about their throwing their pitches together, 13/4 & 4/-, as they intend to take down the side under where Tom Rogers worked. I layed the case before both Capt Rules and they consented at once, that the whole ground be worked at 8/8.* It was a good example of mine captains expressing their concern over bad practice, the miners fighting their corner and the mine manager and senior mine captain agreeing a sensible compromise.

Another case of the captains watching out for fiddling on the part of the tributers was dealt with in September 1823, when a complaint over the behaviour of a pare went right to the purser, Mr William Reynolds, who took decisive action against them. Petherick reported: *Peter Grangey & Rogers & all the whole tote of them were all turned off today by Mr Reynolds for a sett of rogues & vagabonds & the pitch sett anew for 6s/10d in the pound.* It appears that a blatant piece of deception was carried out on the value of the copper ore in the stope, and the tributers were given a higher price than the pitch deserved. The stope where their pitch was located was on North Lode at the 110fm level, and it does not appear to have been the first time that the purser had been involved with Tom Rogers and his mates, for on April 10 Thomas said, *I have been over to Capt Rule's this evening, he told me the business about Rogers & ptrs should be brought before Mr Reynolds on Saturday, and till then they must cease working.* The following day Petherick added: *The line of conduct to pursue with respect to Rogers & Marks will be decided on tomorrow after Mr Reynolds comes here, perhaps I may be wanted on the business.* Tom Rogers had changed his partner, apparently, but not his habits.

The alert mine captain might recognise roguery when there was only a hint of deception. Captain Petherick noted on August 25 something that caused him suspicion. *Wm Richards (Daniel) was saying to me about going with Frankey Rule & ptrs in John Vincent's place, but I think as they were so uncommonly eager to split the pitches, they should remain so, because Frankey & pare have a little ore more than is in their pitch, they want to go back again & in the course of a month we shall have the trouble of separating the pitches once more. Capt Rule Junr is going down here tomorrow.* The tributers, it seems, had originally asked to split neighbouring pitches so that ore could be moved from the lower tribute pitch to the higher. Richards then wanted to reunite the pitches, so that the tributers could benefit from a better price, whilst having available higher grade ore, hopefully unseen by the captains.

The informal way that tribute pitches could sometimes be sett or granted is illustrated by the entry of Captain Petherick for July 28, when a group of tributers approached him to take *John Bennett's old pitch*. As he thought them *pretty good hands for such a place*, provided Captain Thomas had no objection, he said he *will sett it to them*. Captain Thomas gave another example on August 5 1823. *Capt Rule sett two pitches up in the ball today, 10/-*

each – John Vial & his pare is gone in one of them & Wm Pryor & John Jeffrey, Abey Skewes & James Rule in the other, with Wm Tippet & pare – 8 men in a pitch – I have sett John Vial's pitch to Henry Dinnes & ptrs, after they have cleared up their old stuff – Wm Rule & ptrs is going to keep on Abey's pitch for this taking. It seems that after the regular setting day auction, where pitches tended to go to the lowest bidder, the pitches which remained were dealt with less formerly by the manager and his captains.

The Day & Night Book refers to at least 63 individual tributers, some of whom were on tribute all or almost all the time, and were the 'takers', some were tributers mates or partners, and some were occasional tributers.

Development was also a concern to the 'day & night' captain, and supervising the tutworkers an important part of their jobs. The mine captains inspected the various ends being driven, raised or sunk, as well as measuring them for payment and to keep the mine plans up-to-date. They were also concerned about the grade of ore in the end, and if it was a crosscut, they wanted to know when a lode was intersected or if mineralised ground indicated the lode was close. Good examples of this were the constant checks on Trezona's end, on the 145, close to North Valley Shaft. On January 9 Captain Thomas visited the end and reported that *Trezona's end looks much the same.* Four days later Petherick visited Trezona and said the end was not looking so good for copper or tin, but as the *hard stone appears to be nearly all gone* they could lower the price per fathom. On February 19 Petherick mentioned that as soon as Trezona's dirt *was drawn, Stephen Thomas, the halvan man, took possession of it.* There was clearly some ore in it, but not much. On February 21 Thomas again visited the place: *There is some ore & mundick in Trezona's end, which leads me to think we are not far from the lode.* That night Petherick commented that the last time he had visited Trezona's end: *I thought they had cut an eastern part of (the) course, not the right one.* Three days later he suggested to Thomas that he direct Trezona to drive east on the lode he had intersected, but Thomas, not wanting to take responsibility, declined, despite the younger captain having drawn a sketch of the end to illustrate his opinion. On March 3 Captain Thomas measured the end and commented, *There is some good bits of ore in it with a large quantity of mundick.* A week later Petherick again examined the end: *I've been down to North Valley today. Trezona's end* appears to be near the lode by the great variety of substances which compose. Three days later he said the end was *much the same*. The two mine captains continued to inspect Trezona's end through April and May, and the final reference to it was on May 27, when Captain Thomas reported that it was *hard & ugly*.

A typical day inspecting and measuring development ends, was reported in the journal of August 26 1823, by Captain Petherick. *I've been down today & dialed the 100 west of Water Whim to end, then went down to 110 & north thru' the Xcut to North Lodes, down to 118 then west to footway & up to 100 west in Xcut & dialed east to Oppy's end. From thence up to 40, then west down to the 60, then up to the 50 on South Part, and east to Machine to see the new footway, etc. Abraham has altered his plan & now says he can back it up, the west of the shaft appears to be in waste. It will save a great deal of timber if we can back it up.* In the course of this inspection of drives and crosscuts, Petherick climbed down 780 feet from surface to the 100fm level, surveyed the end, climbed down another 60 feet to the 110, inspected the crosscut and pitches at that level, climbed down another 48 feet to the 118 level, walked through another crosscut and climbed the footway (ladder road) back up 108 feet to the 100 level, went through another crosscut and surveyed (*dialed*) and measured to Oppy's end, before climbing up some 360 feet to the 40fm level, then climbed down 120 feet to the 60 level and up again another 60 feet to the 50fm level. He then inspected a new ladder way (*footway*) at Machine Shaft, before climbing to surface, another 480 feet.

Tutworkers driving development ends or crosscuts were not referred to as often in the journal as were the tributers, partly because there was less new ground being opened up at that time than there was normally, and also because mine captains were under constant pressure to increase production. Supervision of tributers was also a more delicate and problematic task than directing, inspecting and measuring tutworkers' ends. However, concern could be expressed if an end was moving too slowly, and such thoughts were expressed by Petherick, on September 17 1823, about the speed that James Hocking & ptrs were moving in their drive on the 100fm level. *I've been down to the 100 on South Lode thinking to mark James Hocking's end, but I'm rather inclined to think that we shall be spared that trouble for this month, as it's rather likely that the 30/- bargain will* last them untill next survey day at the rate they are going on. It was the custom when setting a tutwork contract to agree a certain rate per fathom for so many fathoms, and if that figure was reached before the end of the month, and most tutwork contracts were for a month, the rate would be reset, usually at a lower price. There were many exceptions to this, and particulary if an adit was being driven home it was desirable to offer good money to encourage all speed. Two days later Petherick again mentioned the slow movement of the 100 end, and waxed poetic as he described James Hocking's rate of progress. *Capt Rule has been saying this week about driving an end west from eastward at 80fms level on the South Lode that we have at the 100, south of South Valley. I think it will take James Hocking all this month to compleat his 30/- bargain. If you see them on Monday give them a good rally, they seem to have no more forecast than a grasshopper which sings in the springtime, laughs in autumn & dies in the winter.* Whatever Hocking's problems, Petherick was not sympathetic.

Sometimes tutworkers carried out a variety of tasks on the same contract. Until August 6 John Jenkin & ptrs had been tributers with a pitch in a stope alongside Machine Shaft. The pitch failed when attle from above the level, the 60fm level, ran into it and also endangered the shaft. The enormous run of ground filled a void down to the 134 level. Jenkin and his mates were able to repair the shaft and contain the attle, but a fortnight later they were given a tutwork contract to complete a rise over the 60fm level to the 50 level, and to replace the shaft ladderway which had been destroyed by the run of attle. On the 14th Petherick wrote to Thomas: *I've sett the job to hole to 50 & clear the level & put in footway to Uncle Jemmy Jenkin & pare for £4. They have rose 5 or 6 feet & have not yet holed.* That night Thomas visited the rise and recorded, *I saw Jenkin's men to night. They have holed the rise to the 50 level, it's a good job to have a road in safety.* By the 22nd it was reported that the leading timberman, Abraham, had assisted Jenkin to put in a launder to carry off water and to complete the ladderway between the 60 and 50fm levels.

On December 11 1822 Captain Thomas described a payable piece of ground and suggested that a crosscut be driven on the level below to pick it up. *I have been down thro' the south lodes today. There is a branch of good gray ores, about 4 or 5 inches big, with John Vincent & ptrs & also Mark Terrill*

Captain James Thomas 1778–1867
Mine captain, local Wesleyan preacher and mine adventurer. Uncle to Captain
Charles Thomas, the great manager of Dolcoath. Photograph by William Piper c1860
(Charles Thomas)

Captain John Rule Senior 1751–1834
By 1781 he was a mine captain at Cook's Kitchen. Became Dolcoath manager in 1806 until his death in 1834. Photograph of original oil painting of 1796 (Charles Thomas)

Captain John Rule Junior 1784–1866
Eldest son of John Rule Senior, he was his right hand man until he went to work for John Taylor. Moved to Mexico in 1825 and became famous as 'Mexico Rule'. Photograph of and oil painting by T Boldan c1850 (Charles Thomas)

Captain James Thomas' birthplace
The thatched cottage on the left was built by Jacob Thomas, when he arrived in Bolenowe in the early eighteenth century. Captain James Thomas was born there, and his father William entertained John Wesley there. It was pulled down a hundred years ago. The chapel on the right was used by the Thomas family from the late eighteenth century – it is now a dwelling house. (Charles Thomas)

Captain James Thomas' house in Bolenowe
Captain Thomas built this beatiful house completing it in 1820. He lived there and farmed the land around it until his death. (Charles Thomas)

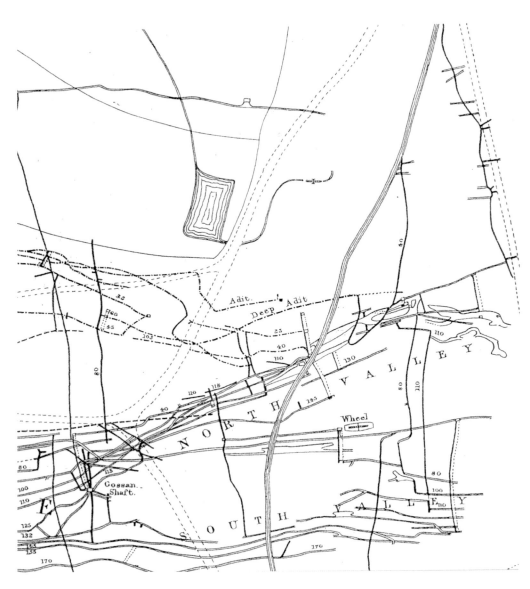

This map shows the Valley Section of Dolcoath with Entral Section. This was the mine in the 1820s when Captains Petherick and Thomas were in charge. (De Le Beche)

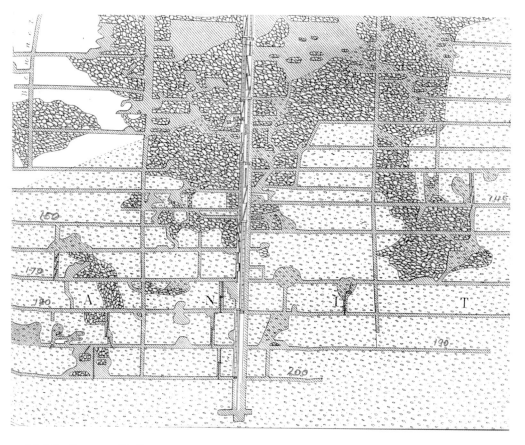

Middle Section (Bullen Garden). The Section shows the lower levels of the mine where a rich tin lode was discovered in 1822 at the 190 and 200 fathom levels. The mine was not deepened beyond this for many years. (De Le Beche)

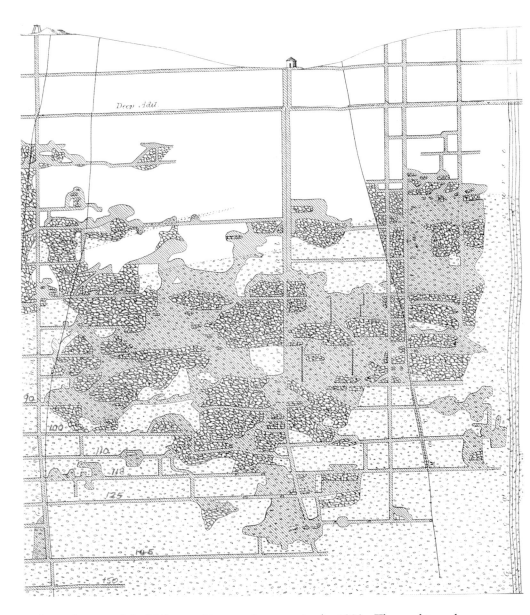

Long Section of the Valley workings as they were in the 1820s. The workings shown are between Gossan Shaft on the west and Water Whim Shaft on the east (De Le Beche)

& ptrs. They are sinking after it under the 100fm level, east and west of Water Whim Shaft. I spoke to Capt Rule about having a + cut at 110 to prove it there. He says we shall have some talk about it on Saturday. This indicates the line between the authority of the mine captain and the manager. The captain could recommend a new crosscut, but it was the manager's decision. On the other hand Thomas was able to makes a decision about the rate to be paid to tutworkers driving a crosscut. January 10 the journal says: *I have also set the + cut east of Water Whim to cut the north branch at £6 per fathom.* Presumably, the manager had agreed to this crosscut already, or Thomas was making a new arrangement with tutworkers who had reached the prescribed target (the extent of their ('bargain') and were finishing off their contract at a new rate per fathom. Another example of the cooperation between captain and manager was described in the January 9 entry, when Thomas wrote: *Went up with Tom Roberts & ptrs and Pascoe & ptrs, they are now throwing out stuff from the + cut and I have fixt the south valley men with them. I was speaking to Capt Rule about setting the job. He told me he thought it the best way for we to talk about it. I give them a certain sume, he thinks about £20 to £25 might do – so I should think, you may just state your oppinion & I will try to settle with them in the morning.* Captain Rule, the manager, gave his opinion and then left it to the two mine captains to decide on the exact figure for the job.

Sometimes, however, the 'day & night' captains made decisions that were properly the manager's, without consulting him. This could be risky. On February 24 Captain Petherick asked Captain Thomas to get John ('Jan') Trezona to *drive east a little on that lode which they have in their end – don't let Capt Rule know anything about it.* Thomas, being somewhat older and less impetuous than the manager's nephew, chose not to do it. *I have not told Trezona & ptrs to drive east as I did not recolect it.* Perhaps he did indeed forget, but more likely he was not as willing to risk the manager's wrath as was the younger man.

Shafts were a constant problem for the mine captains, and keeping them open and in good repair a daily challenge. Kibble ropes and chains broke, whims needed maintenance, and timber sets and boards (*lafts*) in the shafts and stull pieces protecting the shafts, were all in need of continuous monitoring and repair. Ladder roads had to be repaired and rungs (*staves*) replaced, and frequently new ladders were required. All these things were the responsibility of the 'day & night' captain. After night shift on August 7 1823, William Petherick entered in the journal: *Captn James: I'm afraid that the run at Machine Shaft is an ugly job to get at & that it will cost a pretty deal in labour & timber, however, secured it must be, for if we don't keep Machine Shaft open in preference even to the Valley, we shall soon stop of our own accord. Perhaps the timbering of the east side of the shaft with thick lafts & good caseing, similar to the job above the 70 at Valley, should the gunnies be of a moderate size, may be the best, for I understand that the arch above the 60 is crushed in a most dreadful manner & will take an immense quantity of timber to secure it. I should think if the shaft was reared (Glossary) up in this manner as far as the 70, 'twould be a sufficient security against any runs for the future. This though also is at the same time a dangerous & expensive plan, & I think some time should elapse ere it be put in execution. However, I suppose Abraham can tell best about it & in this last respect let him follow his own judgment. Wm Petherick.* The reference to using Machine Shaft for hoisting instead of Valley (North Valley) Shaft, emphasises the fact mentioned by Captain Thomas earlier the same day, that the two shafts were quite close to each other. The location of North Valley Shaft is known, but not the location of Machine Shaft. Stray Park Mine, ¾ of a mile to the west, also had a Machine Shaft.

Measuring, Dialling & Surveying

Both mine captains were proficient in the use of the miners' dial, which was the basic and essential instrument for surveying underground. The earliest dials, some of which were clearly still in use at Dolcoath in the 1820s, had no levelling bubble, but were merely for determining direction. Captain Petherick owned a more sophisticated instrument, which also had in it a level. This is shown by his request to Captain Thomas, who had borrowed the instrument to dial at Bolenowe Mine, for the return of *the dial which you have at Bolenoe with the level in it.* Mine surveying was not a new practice in the 1820s, for Richard Carew, in his *Survey of Cornwall*, written in the 1580s and published in 1602, described the great skill of the mine surveyors as they accurately brought home an adit to the mine 'by compassings and turnings'. William Pryce, in his *Mineralogia Cornubiensis* of 1778, also dealt in some detail with the art of dialling to determine with accuracy where the levels and shafts lay in relation to each other. Captain

Joel Lean is said to have improved the miners' dial in the early nineteenth century, and by the time of the Day & Night Book there were reliable dials with levels available to miners. As we have seen, John Phillips, and undoubtedly others, taught to young miners the use of instruments like the dial.

It seems very likely that the dial used by Petherick and Thomas was of the type made by Robert Dunkin of Penzance. Dunkin was a saddle maker, who patented several inventions in 1813, including 'Instruments for mining, etc'. F. Pigot's *New Commercial Directory* of 1823, decribed Dunkin as a saddler of Market Place, Penzance, and said that he was also a 'mathematical instrument maker'. Under the name Dunkin & James of Penzance, dials with levels were made and sold to miners throughout Cornwall. One such instrument, now owned by Bryan Earl, was designed to be used for levelling, dialling for direction and measuring the angle of dip of a shaft or winze.

There are mentions of them using these instruments on several levels of the mine, including the adit level at Roskear Broase, and the crosscut north from it, the 42fm crosscut, the 70fm level and the 100fm level. They surveyed throughout Valley Section, Roskear Broase, Wheal Susan and Entral. They also dialled at Bolenowe Mine and Parkanbowen Mine. It is possible that Dolcoath Mine drawings, the plans and sections, were usually prepared by a draughtsman or by John Phillips, but the actual surveying fell to the lot of ordinary 'day & night' captains. The plans of Dolcoath reproduced by De La Beche, were probably drawn by Captain John Rule Junior.

Health & Safety

Safety was a major part of the captain's responsibility. When they visited the ends, winzes, shafts and tribute pitches in the stopes, the two captains were as concerned with noting bad ground or other potentially dangerous situations as they were on the grade and quantity of the copper or tin ore. Scores of references in the journal to dangers noted and remedies ordered were made. On December 23 1822 Captain Thomas reported: *I came out thru 110 + cut, thru' Ivey's & Rogers' Pitches, very dangerous places.* The entry of January 13 1823, from Petherick says: *Captn James: I've been down today … Saw Tom Oppey & ptrs, there is very bad ground about the shaft at the 134. Saw Pascoe & ptrs throwing deads like sons of bitches at 118. Went to* examine the state of the stulls up over their west of Valley Shaft at 110 on N(orth) Part & found all the attle from 8 or 10 fms west of the shaft in a sinking state. We quickly decamp'd from there & came back through Iveys pitch on South Part, crawl'd in through a small hole & found the attle in the same state, all sinking. Retreated as quick as possible from these scenes of danger & arrived in Tom Roger's pitch, which is as dangerous as any of them – arrived up at ½ past 2 o'clock, hungry & tired. Will eat all the day bread. Wm Petherick. The following day Petherick reported that he had taken Abraham and Crase, the two senior timbermen in Valley Section, to inspect the stulls over Pascoe's workplace, and although the attle was still sinking, the miners did not believe they were in unusual danger. Notwithstanding, Petherick gave them a bargain for £25 for the task of repairing the stulls, which included payment for timber and 10s tribute for the ore they gained. On June 10 Thomas wrote that he had been through the 110fm level crosscut and examined Benjamin Thomas's pitch. It's all safe.

On March 3 1823 Thomas noted a dangerous situation at Gossan Shaft, which he arranged to be rectified: I was also in the Gossan Shaft at the 40, there is a very dangerous piece of ground and a great deal of attle just ready to come away in the shaft. I ordered Abraham & Sampy Roberts & Wm Thomas to repair it. I have got the ladder put in their old place in the Valley Shaft over 40. Shafts and adjacent stopes, especially where, as in much of Dolcoath, the shaft pillars had been mined away, were in constant need of inspection and remediation. On August 7 1823 James Thomas reported: I have been down today with Abraham & Uncle Jemy Jenkin & ptrs. There is a quantity of stuff fell away from over the 60 in Machine Shaft and filled it about 8 or 10 fms over the 134. It's a good job that Trezona nor D Thomas was not down – we can put that stuff to stull near the Valley – to secure the shaft at the 60 is the principle thing – we shall see about it tomorrow. The road from Valley to Machine over Dinnis's pitch is too bad for any man to go, but we all got up safe. The following day Thomas said: Abraham is to be sent down from the 40 (Machine) thro' the shaft tomorrow, to see what state the ground is in over the 60. I have had a counsel with Capt Rule, etc, about the job. If Abraham thinks it will stand for a few months we may be better able to repair it – but if it's in danger of falling away, we must try to secure it. Richard Pryor's men & John Jenkin with 2 of Adam's will do to assist Abraham about it. I have by Capt Rule's consent sett a bargain to John Trezona & ptrs & Davy Thomas & ptrs to put in timber over the stopes *above the 134 near the Valley, & to put back all the attle that is in the Machine Shaft, which is about 10fms in height – £6 6s.*

Sometimes even the most experienced miners were frightened by falls of ground, and then the mine captains might have to resort to a little psychology or unorthodox persuasion to encourage the nervous man to get on with the job in hand. On 25 March 1823 Petherick reported: *Abraham has been bravely frightened today, a piece of ground came away on him while he was in the couch, but no harm came of it. I have sent Crase & him to take a drop of something to comfort their hearts in order that they may bear it a little more patiently.* The couch appears to have been a sort of platform, suspended in the shaft on ropes or chains, from which repairs were carried out. Two months later Abraham and Crase were again working from the couch suspended in a shaft, when they were *frightened today down in the couch. Some attle fell from under.* Captain Thomas does not say if he offered them some alcohol to restore their spirits, but as it worked the first time, perhaps he did. One week later, on July 1, the unfortunate Abraham had another fright: *Abraham & pare have been down today & got the shaft in course for drawing. There has been another run above the 70 which knocked some of their lights out & I believe it's running still.* This was too much for the timberman and he went off sick. Nearly a month after this third fright, Abraham was still not back at work, and Petherick asked: *How is Abraham? Is he able to come to work yet? Should he have the fear I should be very sorry for him.* It seems the senior timberman had temporarily lost his nerve. By August 25 Abraham was back at his work, although he had not entirely lost his nervousness about falling ground. *I saw Abraham & pare, 'twas 8 o'clock or so when they came up. They have put in the ladder. Some of the south ground has been falling today. Abraham thinks he shall have his head scat away if he don't look sharp.* The danger from falling rocks, was referred to by Thomas Oliver, in his *Autobiography of a Cornish Miner.* He graphically described working on a 'swing stage' in a wide stope, and "while working there I have felt my hair rise through fear when a stone fell from above." Every miner has experienced this and is familiar with the feeling.

Another aspect of safety had to do with the short or long-term health of the miners. On June 20 1823 William Petherick visited the 70fm level west of Entral Shaft, and was disturbed to find that the *sollars* (were) *chaoked &*

(there was) *no air in the end.* The tutworkers, Kitt & ptrs, were warned by Petherick about this state of things and told to clear the sollars and allow the free movement of air. Nearly a fortnight later Petherick again visited the 70fm level end in Entral, and once again the floor sollars were chaoked. He reported: *Sollars all chaoked & end full of stuff, which according to custom Kit promised to clear against I came again. I told him he should not work there any more if he did not be cleaner in his work, and if he was hurted by means of the bad air, he should not be paid for it from the Club.* A floor sollar was a false floor, constructed of timber boards or planks, allowing the air to flow to the end by means of a circuit. The air came down a winze or shaft, and by sealing off the tunnel on the side of the winze farthest from the end, the air flowed toward the end and back along the level beneath the solar. It was usually effective for a short distance, but there are examples of it bringing air to an end hundreds of feet from a shaft or winze.

Accidents relating to ladders were a major problem throughout Cornish mines, especially before man engines and cages were used to take men to and from their workplaces. John Harris described the scores of ladders he had to descend to his workplace, many of them lying at odd angles and some of them poorly fixed. Travelling with a candle for light, slippery rungs, loose ladders and huge drops, all meant that serious injury or death were constantly in attendance whilst climbing up or down the many hundred feet to or from a miner's working level. On 26 February 1823 Richard Rule fell off a ladder whilst ascending to grass after a shift underground at Dolcoath. He had almost reached the surface when a stave of the ladder gave way, plunging him backwards down the shaft to his death. On the night of June 9 1823, James Bennetts, who rejoiced in the nickname, *Patience,* probably in order to distinguish him from a fellow miner of the same name, had a mishap. Captain Petherick stated: *James Bennetts (Patience) in going underground tonight, sprained his side & was obliged to come up again. It was owing to three staves (Glossary) being gone in the second ladder above the 80.* The following day Thomas went to the 80fm level to inspect the pitches there, and commented: *I have put Wm Pryor Junr to make a road to Valley ladder road and when he has done that he will repair the road to the shaft to bring kibbles etc, etc.* Presumably, Pryor was a timberman, or general maintenance man, employed on the 'owners' account'. Working on the kibble road in the shaft, Pryor would have used the ladders there, so the small task of replacing the missing staves would probably have taken place whilst engaged in the other more pressing jobs.

A fortnight after the last entry in the Day & Night Book, the *West Briton* of October 31 1823 reported: *On Tuesday last, as a young man was ascending a ladder in Dolcoath Mine, he fell into the shaft, and was killed on the spot.* Twelve months later another Dolcoath miner, Oliver Rule, also fell from a ladder and was killed. Falling from ladders was a very real problem in deep mines like Dolcoath.

June 9 1823 saw an unusual accident. Captain Thomas wrote: *Uncle Stephen Jeffrey had his head cut in a shocking manner by the Holing Engine. I think so bad a wound as ever I saw. The doctor says he hopes that his scul is not hurt.* Precisely what the *Holing Engine* that so injured the miner, we do not know. It appears likely to have been the miners' name for a device for driving a 'boyer' or drill steel through to hole a shaft or end, or for breaking away the intervening ground between the end and the shaft. 'Uncle' Stephen Jeffery had been engaged in holing a shaft at the 100fm level, and on May 12 Thomas reported that Jeffery and James Oppey had holed the shaft with a 'boyer' or borer. The distance drilled was five feet. On May 15 Thomas visited the 100 end and spoke to Jeffery through the hole. He said that two miners were working from each side and that they were doing a good job. On the 27th of the month Thomas mentioned that Jeffery was delighted that their dirt was being hoisted by *the whim kibble instead of the wins kibble*. Its greater capacity enabled the miners to clear their attle faster than with the smaller kibble. A fortnight later the accident with the 'Holing Engine' occurred. The day after the accident, the less sympathetic Captain Petherick commented: *I am sorry for Uncle Stee to have met with such an accident, but from all the accounts which I have been able to collect this evening, it was his own carelessness.*

On June 11 it was reported to Captain Thomas that *Uncle Step Jeffery is very bad*, but, notwithstanding the seriousness of the wound, the tough older miner was back at work by September 8, when it was reported to Thomas that he was back to work. *Uncle Ste Jeffery has begun to work a little today. I hope he will be able to keep on.* On October 4 Jeffery was demonstrating his return to full fitness, when he skilfully negotiated how he wanted his compensation for being off sick paid to him. Thomas wrote: *I have charged Uncle Step Jeffrey his 20/- subsist today, and not given him any club pay, as he wished to have what he had got on stems now, & to have his months club pay on tutwork pay day.* This series of events tells much about the responsibilities of the mine captain, their attitudes to the miners, of their power to vary the way payments were made and how such things as accident enquiries were dealt with. The older captain was most concerned for the welfare of the miner, but the younger, perhaps more ambitious Petherick, was more concerned with establishing the facts and where blame lay. The older man welcomed back *Uncle Stee*, and even allowing him to have his club paid to him how he wished, the younger made no comment about Jeffery's return.

All the danger to health and safety, however, was not from working underground, and complaints about the affect upon health posed by smoke and fumes from the *burning house* stack were not uncommon. Captain Petherick worked the night shift on the particularly cold night of February 20 1823. He was forced to stay on surface and carry out office duties. *It has been a most dismal night for what with rain falling, wind blowing & cold pinching, I've passed a most uncomfortable night ... O the infernal Burning House smoke, I'm almost choked with it.* The freezing temperature and driving rain would have been bad enough, but the poisonous exhaust from the arsenic calciner chimney would have been enough to cause Petherick to abandon his office responsibilities and go underground for warmth and 'fresh' air. On the night of September 30 Petherick was again confined to the office to bring the *whim drawing* book up to date, and work out what was owed the miners for the stems they had worked. Once again it was a dreadful night: *It's as dark as a pit & most dreadfull flood of rain.* What was worse, however, was the smoke from the burning house. *I've been choked with poison tonight ... I expect to be white against I get home.* At that time the burning houses were used to burn off the unwanted arsenic and sulphide contaminants in the black tin. It was unusual for the arsenic to be salvaged for sale, although as the century progressed, and highly efficient arsenic calciners were introduced, the sale of the poisonous white powder became very important to those mines which could produce it economically.

Notwithstanding the care and attention, with which conscientious mine captains carried out their responsiblities, serious accidents and even fatalities did occur. The journal does not detail any of these fatal accidents, but it does make passing references to the deaths of some of Dolcoath's miners. On January 6 1823 Captain Thomas said: *I saw Henry Vincent Junior – His father's coffin cost 45/- and say for all other expenses on the occasion 15/- or 20/- more. I don't think it would be out of the way – mind to put it in the book.* Apart from the fact that Henry Vincent worked at Dolcoath, and probably was accidentally killed there, we know very little. He lived at Helegan Carne, was aged 59 years, and was buried at Camborne churchyard on the 30 December 1822. It seems likely that his son, Henry Vincent Junior, also worked at the mine. On January 9 1823 Captain Petherick attended the funeral of 'F. Bartle', also a recent employee of the mine. The Camborne Parish Burial Register records that Henry Bartle was buried that day at Camborne. He came from Gwinear Parish and was 32 years old. Petherick said there was *an immense concourse of people present.* He also noted, that, *according to custom* there were two or three females to every male at the funeral. Typically, despite the mournful occasion, Petherick managed to make fun of some of the congregation, especially over the care and attention taken by the females over their attire. *Amongst them I observed Betsy, who I've no doubt can give you a very particular account of all the business so far as concerns frocks, frills, bonnets, stockings, garters, etc, who the mourners were, who was leading & who was not, who was in a fine deal of trouble, & who seemed to take very little notice of it, in short of every little particular incident from stepping in the pig's turds to the parson in his surplice.* It appears that Henry Bartle was killed at the mine, although we have no details.

On the night of January 16 Captain Thomas spoke of the unfortunate death one of their older workers. *I am very sorry to hear of the misfortune that has happened to Ned George. Poor old fellow, his dowsen (Glossary) is all over. It was a great pity that he attempted to come away in such weather – but it's appointed for man once to die.* The weather had turned very cold and the snow was severe at Camborne. The next entry in the journal, for the 20th, Thomas complained: *It was with much dificulty I came here this morning, as the snow was very thick on the ground. They whims could not work for want of water, the leats being filled with snow – some of the men was underground and others could not come.* Where Ned George was going when he succumbed, we cannot discover, but it is apparent he should not have been out in such weather. With no entries in the journal for four days it seems likely that the whole mine was brought to a standstill by the snow.

At the end of the night's report for June 3, James Thomas informed Petherick of the burial of Matthew Harris. *Mathew Harris will be buried tomorrow evening at 6 o'clock.* Harris was the uncle of the poet, John Harris, and in his autobiography he spoke of Matthew seriously damaging their cottage wall by a gunpowder blast, due to his attempting to dry out some gunpowder beside the fire. It appears likely that Matthew's brother, John, was injured in the accident which killed him, for there are several references to Club Money being paid out, sometimes to John and sometimes for Matthew in the days following the funeral. Matthew was buried at Camborne churchyard on 4 June, his age was given in the register as 36 years, and his place of dwelling 'Bolenna' (Bolenowe). It must have been a sad day for Captain Thomas, for he was a friend of the Harris family, being their close neighbour, and, like them, a devout Wesleyan.

On the night of July 2 James Thomas said he intended to go to the funeral of Henry Eva the following day. Eva, from Condurrow, was 21 years old, and was buried at Camborne churchyard. The journal tells nothing about Eva's death, but it appears that he worked at Dolcoath and may have been killed in an accident there. Also on July 2 Petherick made some sarcastic comments about a certain Soddy, who had attended another funeral, at Illogan Church. *There was a grand job of it I understand at Illogan today. Soddy had a new suit of black & a silk hat band.* Whose funeral it was we do not know. Another funeral was attended by Captain Petherick on August 15, but again, there is no information as to whose it was, or whether there was a connection to the mine.

The frequency of certain types of accident at Dolcoath and other Cornish mines, was high-lighted by Dr J.A. Paris in his paper on the desirability of using no-ferrous tamping bars when charging a hole with gunpowder. Paris detailed nearly a hundred such accidents between about 1810 and 1817, and eight of these accidents occurred at Dolcoath Mine. None of the Dolcoath accidents were fatal, but four of them caused the loss of at least one eye, and only two of them were able to return to work afterwards. However, the year of Dr Paris' paper, 1817, saw a fatal accident at Dolcoath involving the use of an iron tamping bar. John Allen was killed and his mate Francis Harris, seriously injured – probably fatally– when the hole they were tamping with an iron bar exploded. (RCG 20.06.1817) Both Captain Thomas and Captain Petherick were employed at the mine during those years, and both were familiar with the type of practice, which led to such horrific accidents.

On the last page of the Day & Night Book, dated the night of October 16 1823, Captain William Petherick made reference to a surprising piece of safety equipment. He wrote: *I quite forgot to have the mouth of the Culverin clean'd up on Tuesday*. A culverin was a long-barrelled cannon, used extensively during the recently ended Napoleonic Wars. In 1828 the *Journal of the Royal Geological Society of Cornwall* explained how the worked-out gunnises at Dolcoath were so wide that loose and dangerous rock had to be brought down by cannon fire. The widest of these stopes were in the Valley section of Dolcoath, where captains Thomas and Petherick were in charge of safety. One can imagine the effect of a cannon being fired by miners, some who undoubtedly had used them in anger in the recent wars, upon the ears of the men involved. The culverin would, undoubtedly, have been effective in bringing down loose and dangerous ground, but what collateral damage the ricocheting cannon balls would have caused upon the more stable rock, is anybody's guess.

TIN MINING AT DOLCOATH

When William Petherick became a mine captain, Dolcoath had been a copper mine for a hundred years, and it was three generations since there had been an underground tin mine in the area. Even the older Captain James Thomas, brought up in Bolenowe, where tin streaming still took place, would have regarded copper as the principal metallic ore of the Camborne mining district. And so it must have been intriguing to these two men, when the report circulated around the mine, that a valuable tin lode had been discovered at the bottom of the mine. The *West Briton* reported the discovery on September 27 1822: "We understand, that there has been lately cut in Dolcoath Mine, a rich copper lode, which is said to be worth one hundred pounds a fathom ... We have also heard, that there has been discovered in the same mine, a rich lode of tin, about two hundred fathoms from surface." Captains Thomas and Petherick, like typical miners, were determined to find out more about this discovery, and three months later Captain Thomas found time to visit the place where the tin was found. He wrote to Petherick on January 9 1823: *I went down this morning with Capt Tregoning in the Middle District, to the 200fm level & 190, saw some good tin, etc, came up to the 145, went to the Valley thru' a level of mud & stuff.* Valley Section was no deeper than the 145fm level, and the description of his walk back to the Valley, through a level deep in mud and debris, indicates that there was no regularly used connection between these sections at the bottom of the mine.

Another reason for Thomas' curiosity was the increasing incidence of tin in the ore in his section. He returned to the Valley and inspected Jan Trezona's end at the 145fm level, and four days later Petherick commented on the fact that that end *is not looking so well for ore (copper) or tin.* On January 16 1823 Captain Petherick, as a forward-looking mine captain, decided to find out more about this unusual white metal. *Nothing new today. They tin samplers have been here & sampled the tin. I staid up from underground to see how they managed it, but 'twas nothing very particular to see or do.* Although the youngster was unimpressed, tin was to prove of increasing importance to the mine as the years went on, and within months he was to be more involved in its assay, valuation and sale.

James Pascoe & ptrs, working as tutworkers on Roarer Lode at the 118fm level, also found tin ore in their lode. Thomas wrote: *I was up with Pascoe & ptrs in the Roarer. I suppose they will make a finish of the job next week. There is a large lode going west, mixt with ore (copper) & tin, but not rich.* It may not have been considered rich when first discovered, but a week later, on February 27, Petherick asserted: *I rather think some of the men who have been clearing out the Roarer will take it for tin. Should they take it, there are two men who would be glad of a place on tutwork.* Pascoe and his mates, appeared likely to come off tutwork and take a tin tribute pitch on Roarer Lode at the 118fm level, their places on tutwork going to others. For them to be so tempted, the quantity and quality of the tin ore must have been sufficient.

Several tributers were producing useful tonnages of tin ore as 1823 progressed, with T. Roberts & ptrs having a copper pitch and a tin pitch, Richard Prideaux & ptrs producing some tin ore and Davy Thomas & ptrs also working a pitch for tin ore, the deeper levels were beginning to show signs of what was to come at Dolcoath. Captain Thomas remarked on April 4, *The tin men seem to work with spirit.* It was as though the novelty of producing something new, gave the miners a renewed impetus. Petherick might have been unimpressed by his introduction to the dark art of tin assaying, but he, more than any other miner at Dolcoath, was eventually to be very grateful for the white metal.

As the year went on the two captains became involved in other aspects of tin. On May 13 Thomas went *to Red River stamps with Capt Robin, about tin,* a week later he remarked *I like to see the whim going smartly, either drawing ore or tin,* and on August 4 he wrote, *I have been with Capt Rule today looking at tin stuff, burning house, fire stamps, etc.* The following day, Petherick remarked: *No drawing tonight, all hands have been working at the burning house about the tin.* This continued until the night of August 6, when it was stated, *They have been mixing the tin very late tonight, & there has been very little drawing.* The two captains' responsibilities soon involved sampling and taking a closer interest in assaying the tin. And they were not the only ones becoming involved in relatively unfamiliar territory, for Captain Robin and Captain Jelbert had to deal with the tin samples and samplers, and Petherick, ever on the look out for a laugh, told Thomas: *Capt Robin is looking as blue as a yellow butterfly on account of the tin samples being sent to him numbered & ticketed like the* (copper) *ore samples.*

In June 1823 Thomas and Petherick gained another task to add to their already full schedules. Captain John Rule, the manager, informed them that they had to visit the various Cornish smelting houses and negotiate good prices for the mine's black tin. On the 13th Thomas informed Petherick: *The tin ticketing took place today, adventurers 10/- tributers just the same. I saw Capt Rule, he says you must go to smelting house tomorrow, to the west, and Capt William Rule. You must without fail call over to Capt Rule's this evening to take your degrees and orders, and you must get a horse, etc. I am ordered to go to Truro & Carlinick, so we shall leave the* (copper) *ores till Monday.* On the 18th William Petherick went to the Penzance smelters and took with him 23 cwt instead of the promised 55 cwt, which so offended the purchaser, Mr Batten, that he took the tin and refused to pay for it. It appears likely that the fault lay with Captain Robin, for Petherick goes on to criticise him for his attitude: *Capt Robin wished to take up the samples today, but I would not let him. He has had a brave noise today about the tin, but he takes it all very easy & careless.*

On August 15 Petherick asked how the tin had gone today, and that night Thomas left a message to say that it had *sold low*. There was a lull in their involvement with selling Dolcoath's tin for six weeks, but on October 3 they were off again. James Thomas reported: *I have just received orders from Capt Rule to go to Truro smelting house tomorrow, so you will settle the subsist, Club, etc.* On the 6th Petherick said: *I'm order'd off to Angarrack & Trellissick smelting houses to know how much they will give over 10 for 20 for the adventurers tin, that being the price I got at Truro, while at Portreath they would not give more than 9½.* This reference to *10 for 20* meant that theoretically, twenty tons of black tin would produce ten tons of white tin (tin metal). If the price obtained was 10 for 20 then the mine would receive half the tin standard price per ton. That night Captain Thomas asked about the price offered by the western smelters, and supposed that the best price would be from Truro. This view was shared the following day by Petherick: *I'm again order'd off for Truro & Calenick on the tin business. I think we shall get 10/- for the tin.* He was right, *Calenick, Trelissick & Chyandour houses* all agreed at *10/- for 20:* a very good price.

The smelting houses mentioned in the journal were spread between Penzance in the west and Truro in the east. Chyandour was situated at Penzance and had been established by the middle of the eighteenth century, mostly to serve the tin mines in West Penwith. It was owned by the Oxnam and Bolitho families, and was active until 1912. Trelissick smelting house, at Hayle, was fairly new when Captain Petherick visited it in October 1823, being started only in 1820. It closed in the middle of the nineteenth century. Angarrack house was one of the first tin smelting houses to use reverbatory furnaces to operate in Cornwall, being established in 1704. It closed in 1881. Portreath was a new and short-lived smelter, starting in 1814, and closing in 1825. It was situated close to the important coal harbour and largely owned by the Williams family. Truro smelter was also quite new in 1823, being built in 1816. Several important families had an interest in the house, including Daubuz, Vigurs, Magor, Turner and Gatley. It finally closed in 1871. Calenick was also near Truro, and like Angarrack it was one of the oldest reverbatory furnace operating smelting houses in Cornwall. It operated between 1711 and 1891, being run by the Bolitho, Daniell and Michell families.

Dolcoath was to remain a copper mine for several more years, but the writing was already on the wall, and its declining status at the copper ticketing, together with its diminishing copper reserves had already served notice that its future did not lie with the red metal but with the increasingly prevalent, white.

BAL MAIDENS

There is no doubt that one of the most interesting areas of study enlightened by this Day & Night Book was the role and character of the early nineteenth century, female, mine surface worker: the bal maiden. Much has been said about them by modern gender historians, and most of it is based upon limited and second-hand sources. The famous essay written by George Henwood in the *Mining Journal*, and included in the excellent *Cornwall's Mines and Miners*, edited by Roger Burt, does the memory of those hardy women no favours. Henwood had risen from a fairly humble background to the status of mine agent, who regularly contributed to the *Mining Journal* articles on mining. He appears to have become a well-meaning, middle-class, do-gooder liberal, with 'improver' ideals and a jaundiced view of the rough and ready, and usually dirty and often foul-mouthed working classes. Henwood's tone is disapproving, smug and patronising. Captain Thomas and Captain Petherick tell a different story, and although, perhaps, to modern minds, an unflattering one, we clearly see female workers who were strong, independent, free-thinking, hard-working and gutsy. They had a raucous sense of humour, a delight in cheap and brightly coloured clothes, a love of the travelling fair and a delightful disrespect for visiting 'toffs' – especially the dignified and sometimes self-important copper company agents. The bal maiden's pride in her ability to compete with the men in her capacity of mineral dresser, is evident in the so-called chant of the Gwennap bal maidens, as quoted by C. C. James in his *History of the Parish of Gwennap* (p.242):

> "I can buddy, and I can rocky,
> And I can walk like a man,
> I can looby and shaky,
> And please the old Jan."

These vernacular expressions all refer to the business of copper sorting and dressing, and every parish had its own variation of them. The 1842

Parliamentary Commission into working conditions of young people, based on enquiries made the previous year, described in some detail the work done by these bal maidens. After the large ore-bearing rocks had been broken by men or youths with 'ragging' hammers (sledgehammers of some 14 lbs weight), girls of sixteen or over would 'riddle' or 'griddle' the ore by means of a sieve-like apparatus. Girls of a similar age would then 'spal' the stone to the size of a man's fist by use of a smaller sledgehammer called a 'spalling' hammer (4lb to 7lb weight). This was usually done inside open-sided 'spalling sheds', although it was frequently done outside, in all weathers. Next, girls of perhaps fifteen years would break the ore smaller by use of lighter hammers called 'cobbing' hammers. The heads on these hammers were quite long and curved away from the handle, rather than the typical backward curve of the pick head. It was thus reduced to gravel sized ore. Mostly, this operation was carried out inside sheds, with the girls seated on stools or the floor. After the 'cobbing' came the most skilled of the bal maidens, who used the 'bucking' hammer, by means of which the ore was reduced to a coarse sand consistency. 'Bucking' involved holding the hammer with both hands and striking and grinding the gravel in one, fairly deft, movement, on an anvil. This last operation was better paid than the other operations, and the women doing this work could be paid up to a shilling a day. The commissioners reported that there were a total of 198 women working on the surface at Dolcoath in 1841, out of a total workforce of 732. The bal maidens far out-numbered the men at surface, the latter numbering only 83, including boys as young as eight years old. There were two little girls of between eight and nine years old, 34 bal maidens between nine and thirteen years, and 74 between thirteen and eighteen years old. A significant majority of the bal maidens at Dolcoath were indeed, maidens, for the average age was very young.

Writers of the 1840s and 1860s described the 'croust' times (mid-day meal break) of these young women. By the 1860s some mines, and Dolcoath was among the most progressive in its attitude to the welfare of its workers, provided warm rooms where the bal maidens could eat their 'croust', which was usually a pasty. Ovens were provided, where up to two-hundred pasties or hoggans could be heated for the girls, and sometimes they would club together to buy a kettle, so that tea could be made for the resting workers. The 1842 Parliamentary Commissioners' report shows that despite the frequent poverty of these women, they were also proud, and if their food was embarrassingly meagre, they would sneak away to eat it in private, perhaps behind a nearby hedge.

Dr A. K. Hamilton Jenkin had a more sympathetic and discerning view of bal maidens than did George Henwood, and his comments on their character are enlightening: "The Cornish bal maidens formed a class of workwomen to themselves, a class, as a whole, shrewd, honest, respectable, and hard-working. Though sometimes rough in speech and generally plain-spoken enough in repartee, as anyone who addressed them disrespectfully soon found, their work brought with it no demoralization of character. In their dress, too, they were clean and neat, and generally very particular about their appearance." Dr Jenkin then quoted the 1842 commissioners' report: "They wrap their legs in woollen bands in winter, and in summer many of them envelop their faces and throats in handkerchiefs to prevent them getting sunburnt, whilst on Sundays and holidays they appear in apparel of a showy and often expensive description." The 'gook', seen occasionally on photographs taken in the second half of the nineteenth century, was worn by many bal maidens to keep the sun off their heads and protruded forward to shade the face. Traditionally, parishes had their own 'gook' design, much as Breton parishes still retain theirs. In some places the maidens wore what was jokingly called 'a yard of cardboard', which consisted of a long piece of cardboard placed across the crown of the head and held in place by a 'curtain' of thin cloth, which protected the back of the neck.

The Cornish love to sing, and undoubtedly their long association with Methodism and its tradition of beautiful community singing, encouraged and helped them to practice their singing. Hamilton Jenkin wrote of the loss to Cornwall of its bal maidens: "Their disappearance has robbed the surface of a Cornish mine of one of its most picturesque and characteristic features; and never again, one supposes, will the sound of them going by singing at six o'clock in the summer mornings be heard in the mining areas."

The Day & Night Book was, of course, written nearly twenty years before the 1842 Parliamentary Report, and conditions and attitudes were somewhat more primitive then. Victorian values, reflected very much in Henwood's account, had not been invented, and the rough and ready eighteenth century attitudes to sex, violence and the law were still universally adhered to. The earliest references to the women working at Dolcoath was by Captain William Petherick on December 18 1822, whilst still waxing philosophical about life and its meaning. Petherick talks of men's interest in knowledge *on different subjects*, whilst women seek it about such things as *the new goods come home at Mr or Mrs. Such a ones new frills, frocks, skirts, shifts, stockings, ell wide, sown print, fast colour wash to a rag, make up the subject of their discourse.* Not very flattering, but then he discerningly says: *Happiness is the pursuit of everyone. Some take pleasure in one thing & some in another, the schoolboy feels more pleasure in a gingerbread coach than the haughty peer in his coach & six, the bal maid enjoys herself more with an ell wide frock, than the peeress does when covered with the diamonds of Golconda at a royal levee.* The bal maidens love of colourful clothes was mentioned again three weeks later, when Petherick described his attendance at the funeral of 'F' (Henry) Bartle. There was an *immense concourse or people present & I believe 2 or 3 females to 1 male according to custom.* Betsy, the account house woman, was also there, and Petherick suggests that Captain Thomas should ask her for the details *of all the business so far as concerns frocks, frills, bonnets, stockings, garters, etc. Who the mourners were, who was leading & who was not, who was in a fine deal of trouble (i.e. weeping) & who seemed to take very little notice of it …* A funeral was a wonderful chance to display the finery the bal maid had spent her meagre surplus cash on. It was not an opportunity to miss!

Another characteristic of the bal maids was referred to by Petherick after reporting on a visit of the copper company's samplers on December 18 1822. *The samplers have been here today … Mr Noel and Mr Provis were here. Mr Provis was desired to put a little snuff on a certain part, by some of our maidens for a very particular purpose.* No Victorian prudery there! Undoubtedly, the bal maidens had the ability to make these middle class gents a little nervous. However, despite the rude suggestion by the women, Petherick was pleased to note, that generally *Our maidens … behaved pretty well all throughout the mine today.* The following day, clearly enjoying the joke, Captain Thomas, the respectable Wesleyan local preacher, asked: *I wish to know why Mr Provis was desired to put a little snuff on a certain part, by our respectable maidens?* There appears to have been no self-righteous condemnation of his fellow mine workers, by the religious Thomas.

Of course, not all bal maids were especially honest, and given the widespread poverty and struggle to survive, it is not surprising that some fell victim to the many temptations all around. On January 16 1823 Petherick commented on a criminal case, which appears to have involved theft from Dolcoath, as two of their men attended the trial as witnesses. *Smith & Henry Vincent are returned. The maid Eudey was convicted. What her sentence is, is not known as yet.* The two Dolcoath men had returned from their 33 mile winter journey from Bodmin Assizes (or 54 mile trip from Launceston) cold and stiff, and they immediately approached Petherick for cash to buy themselves a pint. The account does not say if their request was successful. What Eudey's crime was we do not know, but the law was harsh in those days and she is unlikely to have got off lightly. On the night of April 17 1823 Captain Petherick had an interesting time, which he described in his report to Captain Thomas, in great detail: *Soon after 6 o'clock tonight I observed 5 or 6 maidens here loitering about until at length they went in Spargoe's cobbing house & I saw them tumbling about something, which I could not find out exactly, but on getting a little closer to the window one of them spied me & gave the alarm. Presently, they all came out & ran away under the account house. I went in the bedroom, but could not see them, so I concluded they were gone in the room. I stayed a minute or so & then went out. I walked on pretty quick & when I came down by Bartle's picking tables I saw a girl, whom I know to be Grace Mayne, standing sentry. On my asking her what she was doing there, she said she was waiting for some one or other to come up from underground. I charged her with stealing barrows & anvils, which she denied. Thinking the others were not far off, I walked into the room & was not surprised to see two girls coming down the house very deliberately with an anvil (Glossary) in a new hand barrow marked T.R.30. I thought to have caught the foremost by her – but they dropt the barrow on seeing me, so soon that I was thrown out in my calculation, however, I walked this pare down as far as the fire stamps & then looking on a little further, saw a girl lugging away an anvil under her cloak. Little Jack Burning house & me ran for it & compelled her to drop it. I gave Jack strict orders to give a good look out & if he caught any more to let me know it. Now, all the maidens work at North Roskeere & I think 'twould be necessary for you to enquire into it a little & spale (Glossary) them. I should know them again were I to see them, & if I see them here tomorrow evening I'll be like Capt Jo Odgers, for I'll have four in hand as sure as they're alive, & they shall be grocked to some tune, they may take their oaths to that.* Captain Joe Odgers was a famous (or notorious)

Camborne character who after a series of adventures wrote a highly colourful account of his life. *Grocked* appears to have been a Cornish dialect word of obscure meaning, but which appears to refer to being punished. (Glossary)

What the outcome of the above story was the journal does not say, although there are further hints at the activity of these North Roskear bal maidens. On June 30 Petherick warns Captain Thomas to *be sure to look out for the maidens again tonight*. And on July 21 he rather obscurely asks: *Has that maid bought up the anvil from Wheal Susan? If she has not, I would send a line to Captain Jo about it & send her to the devil with her ass upwards*. This *Captain Jo* was Captain Joseph Vivian, manager of North Roskear Mine, who presumably was the employer of the young woman. It is also of interest that Petherick suggested to Thomas that he spale or fine the thieves, and presumably meant that he ask Captain Vivian to do so.

On August 26 1823 Petherick once again accused the bal maidens of thieving. *The South Valley maidens have stol'n a piece of whim rope today. They are to be discharg'd tomorrow, unless they will confess who stole it*. That night Captain Thomas wrote: *Who is the beauties at the South Valley that has carried of the rope?* On the 28th Petherick commented: *The business is not settled with the maidens about the rope, it's to be left untill next Saturday*. Nearly three weeks later Petherick again returns to the subject of the stolen whim rope, and once again his sarcastic language is seen as he was exasperated by the lack of consistent action against those he believed were the thieves. *I went to take down the maidens' days this afternoon & was very much surprised to find Pascoe's daughter working with Dick Thomas & pare. On my questioning her how she got there, she told (me) one of you had given her leave to go to work, and Capt Rule didn't say that she should not go to work at all. I told her, I should not put down her days until I knew whether Capt Rule & you had given her leave or not. If she has had leave to go to work now, I think the best way will be to pay some one to steal the rope for her & not put us to the trouble of discharging her again for such a short period*. Despite Petherick's anger and sarcasm, Captain Thomas replied that night in calm and reasonable terms: *I saw Pascoe's daughter on Monday when she told me that she had been working for several days at Wh. Bryant, & that she had spoken to Capt Rule and he did not object to her working, so I told her if she went to work with Dick Thomas it should be on the condition of her getting liberty from Capt Rule – so I thought no more about her.*

These two cases tell us much about the attitude of the bal maidens at that time. It confirms their self-confidence and even arrogance, despite being faced with serious charges of theft, which in the 1820s could send them to prison with hard labour, or worse. When the gang of young women from a neighbouring mine were caught thieving by an official of Dolcoath, they did not panic or even seek to escape without their booty, but rather they either sought to 'face it out' and defy the official, or if possible, escape with their loot. The brazen answer of Grace Mayne, (I'm) *waiting for someone or other to come up from underground,* when caught trespassing and clearly standing sentry for her mates, shows little fear of authority and even less respect. When Pascoe's daughter was discharged for being involved with her mates in stealing a valuable whim rope, she did not hesitate to find a job half-a-mile away on the same mine, and confidently approached the mine manager to seek his permission.

Another bal maiden with attitude was Grace Harvey. On July 24 1823 it was reported that she went to the mine Account House and demanded money she said was owed her, and she made her case with great determination. *Grace Harvey was here today discoursing very sharply with Enoch concerning some money which she says Enoch owes her, but which Enoch stoutly denies, & says 'tis Johnson & not him.* Once again, little deference was shown toward the men in authority.

These entries also tell us something of the two mine captains. In the case of the whim rope, Captain Petherick was all fire and brimstone, demanding they all be discharged and protesting when one of them got her job back within three weeks. Captain Thomas, the Wesleyan preacher, shows a kinder and more tolerant attitude. The older man could shrug and get on with his job, while the younger man was raging sarcastically about paying *some one to steal the rope,* as it might save everyone time and trouble. The incident with the North Roskear bal maids and the theft of the anvils and hand barrow, caused Captain Petherick great anger and frustration. He demanded that they be 'spaled' or fined, and that he would ensure they were caught and punished if they returned again. Captain Thomas does not even mention it in his next journal entry. The younger man was furious at the lack of respect shown him and the flaunting of authority and the law, whereas the older man had seen it all before, and realised that *times are hard*, especially for poor bal maidens.

An example of dishonesty, involving fiddling rather than straightforward thieving, was described by Petherick in his entry for the night of August 21 1823. *If you look over Tom Rogers's account, you see what an attempt has been made to impose upon us by Jenny Stone. I knew what she was at altho' I took down the days as she called them over. I've spaled her 5s, which I shall transfer to Capt Robin's material book on Saturday next. 'Tis a strange thing, that we cannot get correct accounts from them. For my part I'll discharge them as fast as I find them out.* Jenny Stone's dishonesty was more than matched by Captain Petherick's outrage. Again, despite the young man's angry entry in the journal, Captain Thomas does not even mention the incident the following day.

That there were among the bal maids some with loose morals and an easy virtue, there can be no doubt, although there is no reason to suppose that such attitudes were normal or more widespread than in society in general. Abraham, the principal timberman at the eastern end of Dolcoath, and the man responsible for maintaining the safety and efficient use of all the whim shafts in the Valley Section, had just completed a most difficult and dangerous job. On September 11 Captain Petherick reported that Abraham was not merely demanding a generous cash payment for the work, but that *Abraham says he shall take a three weeks round among the women after he has finished it.* That night James Thomas replied, with tongue in cheek: *Tell Abraham that I think one week instead of three will do for him, as Sheaby is still able to work & talk – and she has said that if ever she knows Abraham to go with any other women, she will put hot lead in his ear.* On October 4 1823 the subject came up again, and Thomas wrote: *Abraham … was saying today to be sure to mind about the job in Machine Shaft. It was very dangerous work, etc, etc, etc. He has not yet had his fortnight round among the women, and he wants to have some money, etc.* Who ever Sheaby was, it is to be hoped that she did not catch the timberman as he sought just reward for his dangerous work.

Captain Thomas told Petherick a story about *Uncle Jack … swaggering that he had a smart lady yesterday – Abraham & Crase can tell you all the story – he was up all night with her, etc.* There is no hint as to who the *smart lady* was, but as Abraham was in possession of the full facts, and he spent his spare time in pursuit of bal maidens at the Valley, it is likely she was one of them. Some of the surface foremen could wax poetic about the young women working under them, and one August entry says: *Enoch has been repeating a song tonight, about a fair lady who walked out one May morning & 'twas in the month of May, etc.*

The two mine captains felt a sense of responsibility toward the bal maidens who normally worked the copper dressing floors at the Valley. When the weather stopped work or made it difficult, these women were the first to be laid off. On the night of February 19 Petherick wrote: *Shou'd the weather prove bad tomorrow, they will have some trouble to divide the stamps ore ... there has been a host of maidens here today, looking for work. I told them we could do nothing for them & that they must seek for employ themselves, for if once we begin in that line we shall have our hands full of it every sampling.* A few days later the bal maidens were again reduced, and Petherick wrote: *Capt Rule gave Penrose orders today to turn off 2 of his maidens, which he has done.* In March he expressed the hope that the ore recently drawn to surface would produce *a little work to keep the maidens going,* and in June he was anxious to get a damaged shaft quickly repaired *that we may draw as soon as possible to keep the maidens going.* By the following month production was back on an even keel, and the whole surface workforce was working long hours to keep up with the increased tonnage being drawn to surface. On the night of July 9 1823 Petherick said: *There has been a pretty good number of maidens working out of core tonight.* Whether this referred to straight overtime or to working nightshift, cannot be said, but the bal maidens would certainly be glad of the extra money. A hint that the mine did not like women working by night is found in an entry for October 15: *Peggy Bennetts has been to Capt Rule & he has agreed to allow her a man by night & a woman by day, free and clear of all expences & extra charges whatever.* We are not informed about the nature of this work, but it was reported in the context of copper ore sampling, and so it may well have been ordinary dressing floor work.

The teenage bal maidens, like all young women, loved the fair, and they were happy to walk long distances in all weather to attend. On May 20

Petherick wrote: *It's Whitsun Tuesday & Camborne Fair day.* Captain Petherick announced the day with enthusiasm, and that night Captain Thomas was no less excited by the prospect: *I am now going homeward to see who I can find going home from the fair – perhaps I may see some of the Valley lasses.* Petherick obviously enjoyed himself there, for the next day he wrote: *There was a great number of our lasses at the fair, some had shiners* (sweet hearts = Glossary) *& some had not. 'Twas a very full fair & the whole passed off without any accidents.* According to Nicholas Roscarrack, writing in about 1590, this Whitsun Fair was one of three held to celebrate Camborne's original saint, Meriasek. He said the others were Easter week and on November 9. Although Roscarrack refers to 'Whitsun week', it was the Tuesday that was celebrated in Camborne. Whitsuntide was a favoured time for fairs, according to Professor Charles Thomas (A. C. Thomas, *Christian Antiquities of the Parish of Camborne*, p.128), and the Methodists celebrated Whit-Monday, which became a popular occasion for Sunday School 'tea treats' and sea-side outings. A. S. Oates (*Around Helston in the Old days* (1951) p.33) reckoned that Camborne's Whit-Tuesday Fair died out under pressure from the more popular Methodist celebrations of the previous day. The comment by Petherick that the fair *passed off without any accidents*, probably referred to the reputation of the fair as a noisy and even riotous affair. A quarter-of-a-century later the local Methodist superintendent, Thomas Collins, arranged for his Camborne Sunday School scholars to go to Hayle for the day, to avoid a celebration considered unsuitable for children. (A. C. Thomas p.129) When this feeling of disapproval began among Methodists in Camborne, we do not know, but certainly in the early 1820s the Wesleyan preacher, the energetic and 'modern' young mine captain and the young Camborne bal maids, all appeared to enjoy 'the fun of the fair'.

St Meriasek's Feast day was, since medieval times, the first Friday in June. There is no direct mention of the celebration in the journal, but in the entry by Thomas for the Friday night, June 6, he said: *I expect to see you at Camborne in the evening.* This might have been a reference to the Feast, but as there was no accompanying fair, neither man showed any particular interest in it, and presumably, only the churchgoers among the bal maids would have attended for what was essentially a religious celebration.

On June 30 St Peter's Fair was held in Camborne. Charles Thomas believes that it was celebrated locally as an alternative to Midsummer. According to a grant of 1708, St Peter's Fair was a three day affair, 28th to 30th of June, but after 1779 it was reduced to a one day fair, on the 30th June. (Thomas, pp.129, 130) By the later nineteenth century the celebrations had become scandalous, and local clergymen were publicly denouncing the 'disgusting exhibition'. (Thomas, p.130) Presumably, in the 1820s, when Camborne was still a much smaller town, the fair was enjoyed in a quieter way. On July 1 William Petherick told Thomas: *I saw some of our maidens at the fair last night. Some of them I expect got wet & I suppose spoiled their frocks & skirts. Did you see any of them last night?* Thomas replied that night: *I saw some of the Valley maidens last night going home from the fair about 12 o'clock – with some young men – ask of Betsy Webster & Margaret Freeman, what time they got home and what they said when they parted from one another, near Troon – etc, but don't say that I saw them.* The young mine captain seems to have had a healthy interest in the fair sex, and his older colleague was only too happy to encourage him. Whether the *Patience* of Captain Thomas' heavy punning on the subject of a Mr Newton's *excellent discourse* (given at Tuckingmill Wesleyan Chapel on March 19 1823) was indeed the girl friend or intended girl friend of William Petherick, we do not know, but the teasing use of *Patience*, *Wills* and *Jealousy* went on for several days and appears to have been quite pointed. Perhaps the young woman was indeed called Patience Wills, and perhaps she was one of their bal maidens. On August 5 young William Petherick went to Redruth fair, but there is no mention of whom he took there.

Despite difficulties over travelling, these mine workers were prepared to attend fairs, especially larger ones, at considerable distances from Camborne. On May 27 Captain Thomas announced that he intended to go to Penzance on the Thursday, for there was to be a large fair there. Petherick commented: *Monsieur Powell & Company passed through Camborne today on their way to Penzance. When you go there, beware of pickpockets, for they follow Powell go where he will. Please let me know whether you intend going or not … be sure you take care of yourself while at Penzance.* Thomas confirmed that he intended going to Penzance fair the following day, and on May 29 Petherick wrote: *I hope you kept clear of pickpockets at*

Penzance, you had the most wonderfully fine day of it. The parochial nature of these men can be seen in their concern over pickpockets at Penzance fair, when no mention was made of such a problem with fairs at Camborne and Redruth. Nothing was said of their Valley bal maidens travelling to Penzance fair, for presumably such a journey was beyond the means of even the most enthusiastic of their young women.

What does all this tell us about Camborne bal maids of the 1820s? The first thing to remind ourselves of, is the danger of generalisation. The examples of dishonesty among these mine workers should not be construed as indicative of widespread or general dishonesty. The outrageous and lewd conduct of some maidens should not lead us to conclude their behaviour was the norm. The disrespect for authority and lack of deference of some female workers does not mean that such attitudes were typical. The delight in brightly coloured, cheap attire of large numbers of these young women, should not lead us to believe that all or most young, working women of the period were given to such things. The enthusiasm for the visiting fair of many bal maids may not have been shared by all or most women engaged in mine work. Undoubtedly, all of these characteristics existed among a fair proportion of the female surface workers at Dolcoath and the other Cornish copper mines. It is certain that many or most of these characteristics were seen by some of their contemporaries as typical of that class of female worker. For the most part these women were young, unmarried and poor. Their meagre wages helped to support the family home, and any surplus could be spent how they liked, and as we have seen, for many, it went on cheap clothes and having fun. Just as our two mine captains had a shared interest in religion, so many of these young women would have been regular attenders at local churches and chapels. Religions have always had more female than male members, and the many Wesleyan and Methodist revivals of the eighteenth and nineteenth centuries were supported by a disproportionately high number of women, both young and old.

ATTITUDES TO LIFE, MATERIALISM, RELIGION & PHILOSOPHY

As noted above captains Petherick and Thomas were men of strong opinions. Captain James Thomas, as a Wesleyan preacher, had a strong belief in the Bible and in Christian teachings about sin, redemption and salvation. But, he also had other less orthodox views on various matters, as one might expect from a man born and brought up on a remote small farm far from 'educated' society. William Petherick was of a different type, however, and although not lacking religious convictions, he had a more sceptical attitude to local beliefs and superstitions, as well as an independent view on man's (and woman's) place in society and the general scheme of things.

At the beginning of the Day & Night Book Petherick displays definite attitudes to such things as the pursuit of knowledge and happiness, and exposes his prejudice toward, what he sees as, the inconsequential interests of the female of the species. Some of what he says appears obscure to the modern mind, but his drift is plain enough. Some words are unclear and hard to read and the punctuation is mine:

Our Literary Labours Society is always sought by ev'ry one, both male & female. Men seek it for a great variety of purposes, sometimes for a desire to trepan, at other times for information on different subjects. Females seek it in general merely for the sake of (discovering) about the new goods come home at Mr or Mrs, such a ones new frills, frocks, skirts, shifts, stockings, ell wide, sown print, fast colours, wash to a rag, make up the subject of their discourse. Petherick appears to view women as essentially frivolous, shallow creatures, whose main interests are inconsequential, whereas men, by nature are more curious and seek information for a more serious purpose. The use of the word 'trepan' in the above context is interesting. Does Petherick mean men sometimes seek information in order to trap or ensnare the unwary, or is it a more obscure reference to access to the brain, as in trepanning? He occasionally used unusual words as though he intended to impress his older colleague with his erudition, as he did in his introduction to the Day & Night Book.

Petherick then develops the theme of man's reason for being on earth: *So far so good, there is one object answered. It's plain to the most common understanding, that man is placed on this earth as a tributer: he has so long a time to work & then must surrender himself & give an account of the work done. Some have not done breaking their ore before are called on; others have done breaking; others have got it to the shaft; many have got it to (surface), & some few have dressed, sampled & sold it; these we say are cock sure of theirs. Verily, I say unto you, these reap their own reward.* (18 Dec 1822) This miner's analogy is apt, for it identifies the way that some intelligent working class men of the time understood the purpose of life. We are here for a time, we try to make good use of that time, and then, apparently, gain an appropriate reward.

On the universal pursuit of happiness Captain Petherick has this to say: *However, happiness is the pursuit of ev'ry one. Some take pleasure in one thing & some in another: the schoolboy feels more pleasure in a gingerbread coach than the haughty peer in his coach & six. The bal maid enjoys herself more with an ell wide frock than the peeress does when cover'd with the diamonds of Golconda at a Royal Levee. If all are pleased with their own foibles, still its well, provided morality is kept in view, but see how pride, envy, hatred, malice & all uncharitableness creeps in, like a toad with its welling powers, & magnifies innocence into wickedness & vice versa.* Petherick believed that the enjoyment gained from material possessions did not depend upon our personal wealth or social position. The poor schoolboy could gain more from a sweet biscuit than a powerful lord from the display of his wealth, and a lowly bal maid had greater pleasure from her cheap frock than a rich lady could from her expensive finery. However, he warned against the pursuit of happiness through mere possessions, by drawing attention to the evils which come from materialism. He sounds almost like a Wesleyan preacher himself as he identifies the dangers inherent in thinking too much of material things.

Five days later, on the December 23 1823, Captain James Thomas reported a dispute between two pares of tributers: *I have been down today with Vine &*

ptrs & James & ptrs, and heard a great deal of confused talk. One said its so, the other, 'Thee art a liard, etc', but in the end of it, I told them we should put the pitches together. That night William Petherick commented on the dispute: *I hope Vine & ptrs & James & ptrs are contented now their pitches are consolidated. If they fall out any more (we) will call them the Young Consols, as long as they live, move & have their being. Really it's a laughable affair to see & hear a number of men disputing again about a thing which they all agree or say it is worth nothing? It looks as if they want an opportunity to fall out about something merely for the sake of keeping their tongues in it.* The role of the 'day and night' captains is clearly seen in this case. They had to act as arbitrators, as honest brokers in a serious argument over the miners' workplace. The tributer was an independent miner. He was not in the true sense an employee of the company, but was 'self-employed', his own man. As such, he negotiated by bidding, for a pitch of ground in a stope and had a legal right to work it according to the custom of the mine. The authority of the mine captains was such, that they could intervene and impose a settlement on two independent groups of miners, who had fallen out over the boundaries of their pitches. That the miners accepted their ruling was a tribute to the honesty and reputation for fairness of these two mine captains. Petherick's comments about these *Young Consols* indicates that some Cornish miners were not only bitter in their recriminations about each other (*Thee art a liard!*), but determined to continue the argument even when they admitted the ground was worth nothing. The number of such disputes referred to by the captains in the journal show that such attitudes were far from uncommon.

On December 23 Captain Thomas wrote to Captain Petherick: *I saw Capt Rule, he told me we are to have a cake tomorrow afternoon and a little ale – so you will come up to partake of the Christmas Cup.* Petherick replied: *I will come up here tomorrow afternoon 3 o'clock if all be well – I little expected last Christmas where I should be against this.* The mine manager and his senior staff enjoying cakes and ale in the office at Christmas time. Such customs have prevailed until the twenty-first century, but what is unusual, was the deeply personal appreciation for the Christmas celebration by Captain Petherick.

Now Christmass draweth nigh at hand; what a variety of sensations fill the mind of the contemplative being on its approach? The most prominent feature which strikes the imagination is the birth of our saviour, who took the form of man upon him, having the great & noble object in view; the redemption of the whole human race. How & in what manner this was effected there are people pay'd for informing others, as I've no pay myself it is not to be expected that I shou'd here enter into learned disquisition on the subject.

The second part, which forces itself upon us, is the lapse of time (1822 years) since the birth. We can form a pretty correct notion of an hour, of a day, of a month, of a year, but when we come to think on hundreds, how we are lost, poor feeble mortals, we cannot comprehend one century & behold here are 18 of them. Christmass is universally allow'd to be a season of merriment to all who enjoy their health. I think if all be well I shall enjoy this. (Night Dec 23 1822)

In the context of his day William Petherick was not a devout or religious man, and yet here he was expressing deep emotions and profound thoughts on the significance of the birth of Christ, eighteen-hundred years before. He did not claim to be a theologian and indeed he felt inadequate to explain the mystery of Jesus' life being transferred from heaven to earth. He was even a little facetious about the fact that he would not attempt it as he was not paid to do so. Nevertheless, he felt humbled, overawed and deeply moved by the immensity of act. Undoubtedly, his friend and correspondent, James Thomas, would have been better able to explain the manifestation of Jesus, and perhaps he did respond to the younger man's comments, but as Thomas' next entry in the journal was ten days later, we do not have his reply.

It seems that money was never far from the mind of Captain Petherick, and if he was not attempting to save the company money, by checking the payment of stems, tribute money, one-off payments for special jobs or the Club, he was commenting on his personal cash-flow problems. On the night of 21 February 1823, after mentioning on the cost of a particular task, and the fact that the improved copper and tin price would help pay for it, he spoke with some amusement of the copper agents (*'samplers'*) falling out badly, presumably over the value of the parcels of ore they were sampling (*'poor buggers'*). Whilst on the subject of money he added: *I never valued money in my life. It has always been with me as the shaking hands with an old friend. I no sooner receive it than it's all gone, however, joy go with it & two pence.*

In the night of 3 April 1823 Petherick wrote to Captain Thomas urging him to check carefully the debts to ensure that the company was not losing money. *Next Saturday being Tribute Pay Day it wou'd be well if you were to examine the debts lying against our South pares, who take up a pretty deal of money, ev'ry pound being handy in these troublesome times. We must continue to catch all we can, now or never, perhaps, we may say. There's nothing like the time present & we must make the best hand we can of it, while we have it in our power, for opportunity once lost can never be recalled. This is a knock down truth & as plain as a pikestaff.*

On July 29 money was forced once again into William Petherick's mind. He wrote to James Thomas: *I've heard some bad news today concerning the agents' wages in this mine being lowered. I hope 'twill not be the case.* This was not good news for the young mine captain. Precisely how much the day and night captains were paid in 1823 we do not know, but in 1809, the Reverend Richard Warner visited Dolcoath, and he reported that the 'inferior' mine captains were on a salary of 6gns (£6 6s) a month. When, eleven years later (in 1834), Captain Petherick took over as manager on the death of his uncle, his salary rose to an impressive 14½gns (£15 4s 6d) a month.

Between the 17th and 25th March 1823 there was an ongoing discussion about preachers and their sermons. Some of it was humorous and sarcastic and some of the talk was thoughtful and serious. That these busy men took the time to attend such lectures and then discuss them thereafter, tells us something of the way that theological subjects were viewed among the more intelligent working classes, or newly emerging lower middle-classes. On the night of March 17 Petherick wrote: *We had a fine orator at Camborne last night, a Mr Dennis from Crowan. Did you ever see a man attempting to clamber up a bank of sand, gain one fathom & loose two, or trying get over a dry stone hedge when all the hedge tumbled on him? Just in such a situation was the poor fellow last night. All his audience were melted into tears, but 'twas owing to an excess of laughter. To hear him talking about the Harlot of Babylon, the Black Prince & genteel sinners, I thought I should piss my breeches.* Not very kind and not particularly respectful, but at least we gain a flavour of the type of subject popular with some local preachers, and once again, we note the attitude to the wealthy, the aristocratic and the gentry.

The following day, Tuesday the 18th, Captain Thomas replied: *I shall try to get up in time to hear Mr Newton at Tuckingmill at 11 o'clock. I expect you will be there, as you heard so fine orator at Camborne Sunday night.* Thomas underlined the words *so fine orator*. On the Wednesday Thomas confirmed that he had indeed heard Mr Newton, *and a most excellent discourse it was.*

On the 24th Thomas had the chance to discuss Mr Newton's sermon, and he filled his commentary with heavily emphasised double-meaning. *Nothing new tonight – in reading your note this evening I am led to think that wether we live in town or country we shall have need of **Patience**, and if a person has a **Will** (as all certainly have) no doubt but that **Will** is often found to be perverse and stubborn, and you are well aware that **Patience** is quite necessary to prove the **Will** to be good. But, it some times happen before **Patience** can accomplish its design, that **Jealousy** raises an outcry. The storm gathers blackness, and poor **Patience** is oblig'd to hide its head, and the **Will** sometimes left unprov'd, but sometimes prov'd to the satisfaction of boath parties.* No doubt about the theme of Mr Newton's discourse, but little doubt also that the older man was gently ribbing his young colleague. Who was Miss Patience Wills? Where did jealousy come in? The next day Petherick tries a little joke of his own, reminding Thomas that he was married and that *jealous wives* were not always patient. His footnote promises a fuller reply when he has the opportunity. That night Captain Thomas returned to his theme, and this time he is less subtle. *I shall be here at 5 o'clock in the evening. Then I expect to hear something from you about **Wills** & **Patience**, etc, etc. But, you know that a young woman is very enticing – who will presume to say what they will do if they are besett – **Patience** is usefull and **Wills** must be prov'd.*

The above informs us that both men, the local preacher and the more sceptical younger man, had an interest in religious ideas and debate. They both listened to the many new ideas being circulated by the accomplished preachers and those less so. The Methodist system of John Wesley had led and was to continue leading to a great variety of teachings on salvation, sin, alcoholic drink and organisational authority. The Wesleyanism practised in the Camborne district in the 1820s, of which James Thomas was a leading exponent, was not straight-laced or puritanical. References to attractive young women, including the bal maids working under their supervision, are to be found throughout the journal, but neither man, the older married one with wife and children, nor the younger, unmarried man, were self-conscious or embarrassed by their appreciation for these young women.

Occasionally in the journal, the two men used proverbs or common expressions to express their ideas or philosophy on some subject. Typical of these is in Thomas' entry for May 16 1823: *We hear people say sometimes, that no body is found wanting **till** they are gone, but it seems some is not found wanting **when** they are gone.* Who or what incident these wise words refer to, Thomas does not say, but no doubt Petherick knew what he colleague was referring to.

An incident, which graphically demonstrates the contrary attitudes of these two mine captains toward superstition, concerned a miner called Davy Thomas. The ever-confident James Thomas, willing to clutch at any straw which might suggest impending success at his 'baby', Bolenowe Mine, reported in a footnote to his entry of May 27 1823: *I am going home to see what is the best news of Bolenowe Mine. Davy Thomas dreamt of a fine course of ore & tin there.* Now, 'dream lodes' are not as rare as we might think, for even in twentieth century South Crofty, there was such a lode. Arthur Stevens, one of Crofty's mine captains, who was in charge of Robinson's Shaft section during the 1940s, had a recurring dream. He was convinced that a rich lode lay parallel to and just north of No.3 lode on 310 level, east of the north crosscut. His mates merely smiled at his insistence, but one day he persuaded the machinemen driving No.3 eastwards, to drill a round in the end of the cuddy on the north side of their drive, where they stored their gear. Reluctantly, having heard about the 'dream lode', they did so. To everyone's surprise, when the nightshift came in to muck the end, they found that a rich tin lode had been cut. The geologists called it 'No.3 North Branch', but the miners knew it as 'Cap'n Steven's dream lode', and it retained this unofficial name into the 1960s. However, despite similar stories and beliefs in the early nineteenth century, Petherick viewed Thomas' confidence in such things as alarming, and he expressed his opinion quite forcefully. *I hope you found Davey's double dream a reality. Such a thing as that wou'd affront the whole of us to a most uncommon degree. What trouble we should have in taking up the dividends ev'ry month, attending accounts, etc, etc – things too numerous to be particularis'd in a handbill, as the showmen say.* Petherick was offended that Thomas should give credence to such things as dreams, and his sarcasm about the dividends to be paid and the accountings to be held due to the wealth generated by the 'dream lode', were typical of him. He was even more caustic with regard to the over-optimistic hopes of a fellow adventurer in West Wheal Wellington. *What a dreadfull affair has befallen Mr Tippet, poor fellow, what will he do? When you see him, observe his eyes, he is now quite insane & talks in a most incoherent manner of a bunch of ore at West Wheal Wellington. I've been looking out for a place where to confine him, and can find no better place than up in Roskear Broase Old Engine House, where he may amuse himself by calling out to people as they pass by. If Donnithorne were to play the tromblo to him, I shou'd not wonder if he attempted to sing the Bay of Biscay O!* Captain Petherick did not suffer fools gladly, and he had no patience with those who allowed their judgement to be clouded by superstition or their misplaced optimism.

It was toward Captain Thomas' enthusiastic belief in Bolenowe Mine that Captain Petherick directed his most constant sarcasm. On August 5 1823 he wrote: *I march'd off to Redruth Fair & there I learnt that you were home valuing the materials on the mine (Bolenowe) for those noble, grand, spirited & disinterested adventurers C & J Harvey. They have a pretty job to do now to value the immence stock in hand, to calculate the debts, etc. I suppose it will take upwards of five minutes to do it!* On September 17 Petherick was on the theme again: *As soon as Bolenowe is cut rich, J Phillips, Richard Rule & myself are going to Scilly, Dublin, Paris, Cadiz, Pisa & the Isle of Scio & where else I don't know yet.* Thomas' zeal for Bolenowe Mine remained undiminished, and on September 24 he left a note for Petherick: *I wish you wou'd desire John Philips to assay the stuff you see on the desk and see if there is any copper in it – beg him to do it this day, as it came from Bolenowe, not from the + cut south, but from the Engine Shaft. What to make of it I don't know. There appears to be a lode coming in the shaft from the north – fine gossan peach & mundic, & I hope, copper. I shall say but little about it till I see more of it – if there is any copper in it it will be worth something.* Regrettably, his hopes were quickly dashed, for Petherick replied the following day: *The stone you left on the desk, J Philips cou'd not assay, but it was the general opinion of the men & Capt Rule amongst them, that there was no copper in it.* Three weeks later Thomas wrote that he had to get home early the following day, as two adventurers were to visit the mine at Bolenowe, and Petherick could not resist a final dig at his friend: *Be sure you don't cut a course of ore against Mr*

Drake & (the Reverend) Shallcross come up tomorrow, because they wou'd be much affronted as to run away.

Some of the above might be seen as demonstrating the credulity of Thomas and the intolerant scepticism of Petherick, but there is an underlying difference of philosophy also. Thomas, more old-fashioned, was willing to consider instinct and 'signs' as pointing the way toward the discovery of elusive rich copper and tin lodes. His hope in the existence of Davey Thomas' 'dream lode', and his confidence in the existence of copper in a sample which contained good 'signs' (gossan peach and mundic) but no copper values, is evidence of this. Petherick, on the other hand, wanted development to be on the basis of science. His contemptuous dismissal of Davey Thomas' dream and Mr Tippet's *insane* belief in a good copper lode at West Wheal Wellington, was matched by his constant jokes about Thomas' belief in impending wealth at Bolenowe Mine.

A characteristic of many Cornish miners was their fatalism. This stoical belief that what happens was destined to happen is one frequently heard even among modern Cornish miners: 'When it's your time, it's your time!" Sometimes, when a risk is taken underground, and another miner suggests caution, the above response can be heard. This matter-of-fact fatalistic approach was to be seen in Captain Thomas' reaction to the death of an old miner, called Ned George. *I am very sorry to hear the misfortune that has happend to Ned George, poor old fellow. His dowsen is all over. It was a great pity that he attempted to come away in such weather – but, it's appointed for man once to die.* His time was up. We are all going to die, sooner or later. Given the dangerous lives they led, such a philosophy undoubtedly helped them all to cope, and their religious faith helped them keep it in perspective.

Captain Petherick was a practical miner with a determination to move mining practice forward at Dolcoath and to take advantage of new ideas and the advancement of science. In line with this, he and the manager's son, Captain John Rule Junior, were involved in improving ventilation in the stopes and ends, and to that end they measured the air-flow on the levels and in the shafts. They checked the shafts to determine which were up-draft and which were down-draft. They took the temperature of the air, the water and the rock at various levels and under a variety of conditions.

Although having deep religious convictions Petherick was also curious about the earth and its makeup, and undoubtedly, like many of his well-educated contemporaries, he questioned the origins of it all. Thirty years later, Thomas Oliver, also a miner at Dolcoath, expressed his thoughts on the origin of the rock and the mineralised veins within it. In his *Autobiography of a Cornish Miner* Oliver wrote: "In 1855, I was working at Dolcoath at the 220 fathoms level driving a crosscut to cut the North lode which has made the most of the riches of the grand old mine. We, the pare, had cut the lode, and were driving East when one day Captain Tonkin came in and noticed a beautiful vug (a cavity) containing some lovely specimens of rock crystals; he desired me to save a piece for him, which I did. We entered into a discussion on the origin of lodes. I asked him what he thought about it. 'O!' he said, 'they were made when the earth and the heavens were created, about six thousand years ago.' I said 'more than six million years ago.' Captain Tonkin was a local preacher, and had been a schoolmaster before he became a mine agent. A short time after this conversation Captain Tonkin went to London for the first time, and he visited the British Museum, and there he saw fossils of animals that lived many millions of years ago. After he came back from London he came where I was working, and the conversation was on the same subject, viz:, the origin of lodes. He said, 'I am converted to your belief. The old book says, in the beginning God created the heavens and the earth, and no one knows when the beginning was.' " Oliver was deeply religious and spent many years as a Methodist local preacher, and it is worth noting that the interest of these men in science and what it had to tell them, in no way affected their firmly held religious convictions. It is also worth noting that the above conversation took place in 1855, some four years before Charles Darwin published his *The Origin of Species*, in 1859. (Thomas Oliver *Autobiography of a Cornish Miner* (1912, Camborne).

THE CAPTAINS' USE OF THE ENGLISH LANGUAGE

Related to the philosophical and religious thinking of Thomas and Petherick was their use of language. As noted above, their choice of words was generally colourful and they habitually used strong language. Blasphemy was not used by either of them, and given their beliefs and ideas, that is not surprising, but vulgarity and expressions verging on the obscene were to be found. Thomas, as one might expect, was the more restrained in his language, but Petherick was frequently quite uninhibited in the words he used. Remembering the rudimentary and extremely limited education enjoyed by these two men, and taking into account their lives working among rough and ready miners, where restraint in expressing themselves would have been rare, it is hardly surprising that swear words and references to the human body using Anglo-Saxon expressions regularly occur. However, we also find extensive use of figurative language in describing things, and metaphors, allegory and simile all find their place in the way they wrote. Simile, particularly, was a favourite literary device of Petherick.

Petherick was given to humorous vulgarity in his speech and the many examples to be found in the journal show little interest in polite euphemism. His references to parts of the human body and to bodily functions were probably typical of the daily speech of his contemporaries and workmates. In the introductory comments he quotes an *old song*, the chorus of which runs: *I do not shite nor thick nor thin, but in the middling way.* This sounds typical of the chorus' of many rugby songs, and although vulgar, it expresses the point he was making about plain speaking. A few lines on, Petherick uses the interesting similes of the *Tail of a Comet* together with the way a lady breaks wind: *It's time to finish this dedication, both descriptive and sentimental. For I'm sure if this subject has not been drawn out like the Tail of a Comet, at least it's drawn out like a lady's fart, that it to say, it's brought to a very fine point.* He again referred to flatulence on April 7 1823, when he visited the Deep Adit at Martins Shaft: *I stay'd there while they put off a hole. It rattled in the adit like a good peas fart.* The sound of blasting a shothole in a narrow tunnel can indeed make the type of sound mentioned by Petherick.

A part of the human body which gave Petherick and Thomas endless opportunities for humour, was the anus. It is of interest that although the word 'ass' was used a couple of times, the writers appeared conscious of its perceived vulgarity. The first reference, 18 December 1822, speaks of putting *a little snuff on a **certain part*** of Mr Noal, the sampler, by the bal maidens. The euphemism was repeated by Thomas the following day, when he requested, *I wish to know why Mr Provis was desired to put a little snuff on a **certain part**, by our respectable maidens?* On 9 May 1823 Petherick used the word 'ass', but then, either he or another party, tried to obliterate it. *Abram has the most violent shits* (crossed out), *he says the hole* (crossed out) *of his ass* (crossed out) *is so sore he can hardly suffer.* Given subsequent entries, it seems certain that the wording was censored by someone else, who came across the words and attempted to obliterate them. Petherick himself, however, did try to avoid writing the potentially offending word on another occasion. On June 18 1823, whilst speaking of the need to put a little life into the unfortunate Captain Kit Robin, he wrote: *He takes it very easy & careless, wou'd it not do him some good if we were to put a little Cayenne Pepper in the hole of his ...* His meaning was plain, but Petherick sought to avoid writing the word. On the night of July 21 he was not so coy. His frustration over the delay and reluctance to deal with the thieving bal maids, caused him to react: *Has that maid brought up the anvil from Wheal Susan? If she has not, I wou'd send a line to Capt Jo* (Vivian) *about it, & send her to the devil with her ass upwards.* On September 9 Petherick used the word as part of a simile. He wrote that the rock on the 42fm level was *as hard as the devil's ass.* Another, slightly different reference to the anus was used by Petherick in a simile about the facial expression of one of the miners, who was sceptical about the origin of a rock sample. *Uncle Stee Jefferey, whose mouth was curl'd up like the furt of an ox, when he pinches off the last bit.* A furt is a Cornish dialect word for a or bull's or cow's anus. To men who lived among farms and worked on them during their spare time, this was a very appropriate simile, and the word was still used among miners into the 1990s.

References to excrement are also found in these entries, usually in a humorous context. We noted the song chorus where it was mentioned, and a month later, on 9 January 1823, after attending a miner's funeral, Petherick made a joke about the preoccupation of some people for all the details of the ceremony. He suggests that Thomas asks the Account House lady, Betsy, for a complete description of what the women were wearing, who was upset and who was unmoved, who took a lead and who followed on, and then concludes: *In short of every little particular incident, from stepping in the pig's turds to the parson in his surplice.* Irreverent but funny. The reference above, to Abram having a bad attack of diarrhoea, which left his anus very sore, and where the words are almost obliterated, is on the same page as another mention. Captain Petherick had visited old Captain Tucker, at Wheal Francis Mine, and he reported part of the conversation he had with him. Angry at some unknown person who had informed on him, Tucker used the most extreme language: *Some damn'd infernal bugger or other must have told them of it, who deserv'd to have his mouth stuff'd with turd a fortnight old & condemned afterwards to have the pox to such a degree as for his limbs to drop off one by one.* The language was colourful and extreme, but the old man was clearly not one to cross.

Another quite different type of reference to excrement was to be found in the entry for May 29 1823, where Petherick talks of the problems which followed on from reducing the number of pitches, due to either the lower copper standard or the dropping off of ore values in the stopes. *I've been Entral today & told them all not to be frightened if their places were stopp'd on Saturday … What shall us do respecting James Oppy & pare. It appears to me that next month they will be oblig'd to shit small turds.* This proverbial Cornish saying refers to the tightening of belts and having less food to eat. Another Cornish expression was used by Petherick on February 20, when he spoke of Captain Robin's discomfort over his failure to correctly estimate the weight of ore he was sampling: *I found Capt Robin looking like one who had been eaten & shitten again in consequence of not being able to tell what weight to put on the scales.* This use of humorous vulgarity was noted earlier when Petherick's attendance at a lecture was reported on. Again he used a common expression, and one still widely used. As the speaker struggled to explain about the *Harlots of Babylon, the Black Prince & Genteel sinners,* Petherick was laughing so much, *I thought I shou'd piss my breeches.*

A favourite swear word of Petherick's appears to have been 'bugger'. He uses it in different ways and not always aggressively. On February 21 1823 he refers to a noisy disagreement between the samplers, and sounds quite sympathetic in his use of the word. *There has been a dreadfull falling out between the samplers, poor buggers, let them get pleas'd again as soon as they may.* His next use of it was when telling of Captain Tucker's outburst – *some damned infernal bugger.* On June 9 1823 Petherick uses the word in anger: *The fire stamps has been idle until 11 o'clock & no smith to be found to make a cutter. Spale the bugger 20s/-.* It appears to have been the normal swear word for all purposes, as, indeed, among mine workers, it has remained.

A great variety of colourful expressions were used throughout the Day & Night Book. These include,*stiff as a poker; tight as murder; big as bull's beef; murder'd or served some ugly trick; bust your guts* (through over-eating); *grocked to some tune; like Capt Joe Odgers ... I'll have four in hand* (reference to famous/notorious local character who wrote his life story); *as notorious as the sun at noon day; rogues and vagabonds; the whole tote of them; looking as blue as a yellow butterfly; should go and cut pudding turf; deads like Sons of bitches; in the dog watch; put hot lead in his ear; no more forecast than a grasshopper which sings in the springtime, laughs in the autumn and dies in the winter; knock down truth & as plain as a pike staff* and *dark as a pit.*

Although undoubtedly using local expressions and dialect in their writings, Thomas and Petherick spoke for the most part in 'modern' English of their day. Occasionally use of the word 'us' instead of 'we' is found in the journal, as in the entry for the night of April 8 1823: *I shou'd think us was to be murder'd ...* It appears that 'us' has been changed to 'I' and then to 'we', perhaps conscious that it was old-fashioned. The reference above to James Oppy & pare also uses the expression: *What shall us do respecting James Oppy.* Another colloquialism was used on that page: *I told them not to be frightened if their places were stopp'd.* This use of frightened instead of surprised is still heard in west Cornwall. On May 15 Petherick says: *somebody else shou'd have left me know.* Left me know instead of let me know, again is still used in west Cornwall. Belong is a word used in an unusual way in Cornwall, as on March 14, when Captain Thomas wrote: *I belong here stem times.* 'I belong to be here' or similar, remains in local usage. Although quoting the words of miners in dispute with each other, Thomas uses really old-fashioned expressions on 23 December 1822: *Thee art a liard!* An attempt was made to scratch out the 'd' on liard, but it remains clearly visible. Local people in the mining areas occasionally still use the word liar with a 'd' on the end. A famous expression of Howard Mankee, a mine captain at South Crofty until the mid-1980s, was: *A man what tells lies is a liard!*

Sarcasm, strong language, colourful expressions, local proverbs, vulgarity and obscenity, are all found in this Day & Night Book. Anger, abuse and threatening language are also there: *Soddy ... will kick you in the shaft ... and W Rule he will kick to hell!* The smith failing to do his job: *Spale* (fine) *the bugger 20s/-.* The bal maid who fails to return a stolen anvil: *Send her to the devil.*

NEIGHBOURING MINES

During the course of their work captains Thomas and Petherick visited many local mines. Over twenty copper mines are mentioned in the text, with one or two, like Bolenowe and West Wheal Wellington, being mentioned frequently. Mines such as Wheal Susan and Stray Park had become part of Dolcoath Mine, but are referred to as distinct sections of the mine, as are Entral, Wheal Bryant and Roskear Broase, all, originally, separate mines.

On December 18 1822 Captain Thomas was at South Wheal Harmony, on the northern side of Redruth, and he reported: *Mr Pendarves, Messers Prades, Mr Knapp, Mr Knight, etc, etc, were at South Wheal Harmony today – all in very good spirits about the lodes there – Mr Prade has taken some shares with it and they are very well pleased with the sett of Advrs that I produced.* This casts Captain Thomas in the role of mine promoter, for he seemed to have been acting as some sort of agent for the mine. Mr Pendarves of Pendarves, Camborne, was an important landowner and mineral lord, who had long held shares in mines at North Downs, Redruth. Mr Praed ('Prade') of Trevethoe, Lelant, was also an important landowner and mineral lord, being involved with East Wheal Crofty and other local mines. Mr Knapp owned Knapp's Hotel in Camborne, and was a friend and colleague of both Captain Thomas and Captain Petherick, who stood godfather to one of his children. Mr Knight was a Camborne man, who appears to have been a local mine adventurer.

On the night of February 21 1823 William Petherick wrote: *I've been down in Wheal Francis today. I saw the old Captain Tucker …* Wheal Francis lay on the tenement of Camborne Veor, just to the west of Camborne railway station and Camborne Vean Mine. Petherick was there to share some gossip with the old man, about a matter of mutual concern. On May 9 he visited Tucker again at Wheal Francis, and it appears to have been another social visit to bring Tucker up to date with the problem they had discussed in February. On September 24 Petherick once again said he intended to go to Wheal Francis, but this time it seems he went for the two-monthly account. Neither Thomas nor Petherick appear to have had a professional interest in Wheal Francis. They went to visit old Captain Tucker, who was an irascible, foul-mouthed but entertaining host, who shared some of their prejudices and opinions.

On 26 February 1823 Captain Thomas reported: *I was requested today to attend a Meeting of Wh Providence advrs at Mr Knapps. I of course attended and found Messers Knapp, Jeffrey, Tippett, Hocking, Henry Reynolds, etc, etc. Had a glass or two of Hollans (Holland Gin) & water and came here.* The Wheal Providence Thomas spoke of was probably the one which lay on the south side of Tincroft Mine, along the northern flank of Carnarthen. It eventually formed part of South Tincroft, one of the constituents of Carn Brea Mine. In the 1820s Wheal Providence was a small mine exploiting a single lode to no great depth. Whether Thomas went as an adventurer or just for his experience and expert opinion, we do not know. Another mine of the same name was in Redruth and appeared in the records between 1819 and 1825. It is just possible that it was this short-lived mine that Thomas attended in 1823. (AKHJ vol 3/28)

Camborne Vean Mine, immediately to the west of Stray Park Mine, was visited fairly regularly by Captain Petherick. He seems to have been involved in surveying there, for although his attendance on survey days could imply involvement in setting pitches, his comments show that he usually went underground when he visited the mine. Perhaps his skill with his dial and level was employed by the management there. Not all small mines employed captains with the necessary training to carry out complicated surveys and draw accurate plans and sections. Some such mines probably did not even own a dial. On March 26 Petherick attended *Camborne Vean Survey*, on May 30 he again went to *C. Vean Survey day*, and this time after coming to surface, he enjoyed a formal dinner there. On July 10 he said he had been underground at Camborne Vean, and, apparently, left his underground clothes there. A fortnight later he went there again. *Ask Betsy for my jacket & trowsers & send them up to C. Vean & my shoes, etc.* He wrote to Thomas: *Tomorrow I shall be at C.Vean according to custom.* As he needed his underground clothes he was clearly surveying underground there. On August 29 Petherick was again surveying at Camborne Vean. It would be of interest to know whether Petherick carried out this regular surveying with the permission of Captain Rule or at his request. Just how much independent work a mine captain could carry out for other employers we do not know. Presumably, every mine and every mine manager had their own arrangements and rules. One example of Petherick being ordered by Captain Rule to carry out a survey at another mine was at Parkenbowen Mine, situated where Ennys Road and Tehidy Road meet in Camborne. On February 24 1823 Petherick wrote: *Captn Rule wishes me to go underground tomorrow at Parkenbowen, to dial some of the ends, as it's suppos'd she will cease working on Friday next & the plan must be finish'd by that time.* Parkenbowen or Parkanbowan, was a small mine which lay to the west of Wheal Chance and Wheal Gerry. It eventually became part of South Roskear Mine. During the eighteenth century Parkanbowan was one of several small copper mines, with Weeth Mine, Wellington and De Dunstanville mines all adjacent to the west and south-west.

Captain Petherick was an adventurer in West Wheal Wellington, and he appears to have been quite proud of it. On April 23 he said: *I am going home in order to meet my brother adventurers in West Wheal Wellington.* A fortnight later he wrote: *I'm gone home this afternoon to go to W.W.Wellington with Messers Jefferey & Tippett.* It appears that this was a new adventure, for on June 3 he announced: *This evening if all be well, we shall Christen West Wheal Wellington Account House.* Despite his delight at being an adventurer in a new mine, Petherick's natural caution did not protect a fellow adventurer from his sarcastic tongue, when the said adventurer, Mr Tippett, showed undue optimism about the mine's prospects. Tippett, *is now quite insane & talks in a most incoherent manner of a bunch of ore at W.W.Wellington.* Petherick suggested that his fellow shareholder be confined somewhere secure. The final mention of West Wheal Wellington indicates that a Captain Skinner was running the mine. Petherick spoke, on July 30 1823, of his being taken down the mine by Captain Skinner, who had also visited Bolenowe Mine for Captain Thomas, presumably to give his opinion on its prospects.

Mine sales were of great interest to mine captains, for new and second-hand gear was always in demand to replace worn out machinery or improve the efficiency of the mine. Sometimes these two mine captains went on their own initiative to these sales, sometimes they were sent by the manager and at other times by the mine engineers. For both men, also, there was the need to buy gear for the mines they had a separate interest in. For Thomas this was Bolenowe Mine and for Petherick it was West Wheal Wellington. On May 1 1823 Captain Petherick wrote: *I rather think I shall go to the Wheal Breage sale tomorrow*. Whether he bought anything is not stated, not is the reason for his interest. He decision appears to have been on a whim. Perhaps he was looking for gear for West Wheal Wellington. Wheal Breage was an ancient mine on the eastern flanks of Tregonning and Godolphin hills, adjacent to Great Work, which it sometimes formed a part of.

In the entry for the night of August 25 Captain Thomas said: *I shall ride over to Crenver tomorrow*. The following day Petherick identified the mine Thomas had visited: *How did you get on at W Abram sale today? Did you buy anything?* That night Thomas replied: *I was at Wh'll Abram, did not buy anything. Nothing but engines & whims offerd for sale. Very few sold*. Wheal Abraham was a large and important mine at Crenver, in the parish of Crowan. It was known for most of the nineteenth century as Crenver & Wheal Abraham. It experienced difficulties in the 1820s, after a long and productive period, closing down in 1825. Thereafter, it had several periods of activity until it closed in the 1870s, by which time it was producing tin as well as copper.

Whilst Captain Thomas was checking Wheal Abraham for gear, one of the mine engineers, Richard Jeffery, requested him to go to a sale at Wheal Neptune, and the following day (August 27) he reported: *Nothing at W. Neptune worth our notice*. Wheal Neptune was situated on the cliffs in Perranuthnoe Parish. It was a very ancient mine, and although not large, it was at times quite productive, working for both copper and tin.

The last mine sale referred to in the Day & Night Book was at Penberthy Crofts Mine. In his entry for the night of September 8 1823, James Thomas wrote: *I have been at Penberthy Crofts today, and brought a few fms of Rods and some oak for lentels for Engine house – I think very reasonable*. It seems likely that Thomas bought the pumping rods and oak for door or window lintels for an enginehouse at his Bolenowe Mine. He was at that time buying parts for a pumping engine for Bolenowe, and he would need both pitwork and a house for the engine. Penberthy Crofts, in St Hilary Parish, was an old mine when Thomas visited it. During the period 1818–25 it sold 8,697 tons of copper ore for £49,291, as well as sixty tons of black tin. It later worked with Great Wheal Fortune. It continued to produce tin until the early years of the twentieth century.

On June 9 Captain Thomas told Petherick: *I was not at Camborn on Saturday. Mr Rob Bennetts call'd on me to go with him to W Foster – were we din'd and afterward had some good punch, etc.* Petherick responded by saying he had heard that Captain Thomas had arranged to go to London with Bennetts, and assured the older man that he would hold the fort in his absence. What Thomas' connection with Wheal Foster we are not told. It seems likely that it was attending an accounting dinner, because he refers to having dined and been given *some good punch.* It is not likely that dinner and punch would have been available on a Saturday unless it was the mine's accounting day. The journal mentions other examples of the two-monthly accounting days being on Saturdays. Wheal Foster was a small mine in the parish of Wendron, and if Robert Bennetts called on Thomas on his way there, they would not have had far to go, for his small farm at Bolenowe was close to the parish boundary with Wendron.

Among the neighbouring mines to Dolcoath, four were referred to by captains Petherick and Thomas in their Day & Night Book. They were North and South Roskear, East Wheal Crofty and Cooks Kitchen. In his report on the night of April 17 1923, when Captain Petherick caught the bal maids red handed as they stole the bucking anvils and hand barrow, he commented that *all these maidens work at North Roskeere.* He referred again to the theft of the anvils on July 21, when he asked Captain Thomas if the *maid has bought up the anvil from Wheal Susan.* If not he felt that Thomas should report it to 'Capt'n Jo', who was Captain Joseph Vivian, manager of both North and South Roskear mines. James Thomas had referred to Vivian the same day, when he spoke of engine parts he wanted to buy for Bolenowe, and added: *Captain Joe from S. Roskear was waiting to accept if I refused.* North and South Roskear mines were large and relatively important copper mines at the time, and Joseph Vivian, who was of the great Camborne mining dynasty of that name, was an extremely important and highly respected mine manager. He later became manager of East Wheal Crofty, which, in the 1830s, was the largest mine in the Camborne-Illogan area. William Petherick visited East Wheal Crofty twice in 1823, on June 3 and on July 29. The first entry states: *I've been down to East W. Crofty today with Cousin W'm Rule. They have a very fine lode there.* The July entry merely said that he had been down East Wheal Crofty that day.

Cooks Kitchen lay on the eastern boundary of Dolcoath and shared its Deep Adit. Both mines, as well as other mines along the adit, were responsible for maintenance of the adit within their setts. Cooks Kitchen adit men had neglected their part of the adit, and Captain Petherick was not pleased, especially when Captain Rule told him to pay his men to do the job which should have been done by Cooks Kitchen. Angrily, Petherick wrote (September 13): *Capt Rule was saying that we must look after the deep adit & give Abram 2/6 a stem for going down there. Cooks Kitchen people have neglected to go down there. He seem'd to talk as if we were to have nothing for it, but I don't know that we should do it for nothing ... any more than other people.* Cooks Kitchen and Dolcoath had the same mineral and landlord, and often shared the same pursers and other aspects of their management. It is possible that Captain Rule was just being diplomatic in not causing a fuss over his neighbour's neglect of the Deep Adit system. Good relations in local politics made sense.

DOLCOATH COPPER MINE, CAMBORNE, CORNWALL.

Dolcoath Copper Mine in the times of Captains Petherick and Thomas. This engraving by T. Allom (1831) shows men, boys and bal maidens performing several tasks at the shaft head (Royal Institution of Cornwall)

A group of nineteenth century Camborne bal maidens (Royal Institution of Cornwall)

Capt Will/

It is not now my task, to defend the
cause of the proprietors of this work
against the unfair attempts of any
individuals who may endeavour to
supplant it in the publick esteem

as its dedicated to our noble
Selves. — Knights of the Beef stew
& steaks &c &c &c ———

I have been down thro the south
lodes to day. there is a branch
of good gray ores about 4 or 5 Inch
big with John Vincent &c &c & also
Mark Terrill &c &c they are sinking
after it under the 100 fm level, &c
and West of W Whim shaft. I spoke to
Capt Rule about having a + cut at 114 &
prove it there, he says we shall have
some talk about it on Saturday, —
I want to be home to morrow abt
my garden before the frost sett in if y
will be so good as stay for me. there
a bit of fresh pork for a steak for
supper. and some salt pork for breakfast
so you will not want meat.
make the men bring down them Ores.

Jas Thomas

The Day and Night Book – 11 December 1822

Captⁿ James

I've been down to day Tregona's
End is not looking so well for ore or tin but
the Ground is far better if it holds untill
Survey day as it is now we must lower
then price Considerably the hard stone appears
to be nearly all gone saw Tomossy &c
there is very bad ground about the shaft
at the 13^f Saw Pascoe &c throwing deads
like sons of bitches at 118 went to Examine
the state of the stulls up over them west
of Valley Shaft at 110 on N Part & found all
the attle from 8 or 10 fms west of the shaft
In a sinking State we quickly decamp'd
from there & Came back through heys pitch
on South part Crawl'd in through a small
Hole & found the attle in the same state
all Sinking retreated as quick as possible
from these Scenes of danger & arriv'd on to
Rogers's pitch which is as dangerous as any of
them — arriv'd up at ¼ past 2 OClock
Hungry & tired Will eat all the dry Bread

Wm Petherick

The Day and Night Book – 13 January 1823

Capt Will/

I have made up the drawing to
night. – I made out the stem bills
as you did not leave any record
of what has transpired to day
I concluded that you were gone
with cousen William to have a
game of cards or something else
but as you observd in the last
page that morality ought to be
kept in view. I hope that my
conjectures are groundless – and
that you spent the evening in
a very profitable & becoming
manner, I wish to know why
Mr Provis was desird to put a little
snuff on a certain part by our
respectable maidens —

Yours &c Jack Thomas

19th N.

The Day and Night Book – night of 19 January 1823

night 3rd —

Capn Wills/

I dont know any thing more to charge
to the Tributers — I saw Sams Roberts &
and I have some Timber & Boards to charge
to them but as I have not measured them
I wish you would charge April stems
&c and the other can be settled another
time — I had promisd Hy Davey & something
for taking up water & for Ladder & so I have
charg'd 25/ — Steh Vine was saying
he took a pitch at Entral, I call'd on him
this evening as I wanted a man at Bolenow
and he told me he would go only for me
to speake to you about it — I beleive the
pitch is not of much consequence —
I want to go to Siney Parish, to morrow
I shall not be here very early in the
evening — Friday evening will do
to make up our Books —
Mathew Harris will bee buried tomorrow
evening at 6 oclock —

James Thomas

The Day and Night Book– night of 3 June 1823

26 August 1823

Capt James

I've been down to day & Dial'd the 100 west of WWhim to end then went down to 110 & North thro the X Cut to North Lode. down to 118 then west to footway Hy to 100 went in X Cut & Dial'd East to opp ys End from thence up to 40 then went down to the 60 then up to the 50 on s' Part & East to Machine to see the new footway & as Abraham has alterd his plan & now says he can back it up the west of the shaft appears to be the wast It will save a great deal of timber if we Can back it up & Cap tn Rule says you must go to penam to morrow & take out 7 a 8 pieces of the largest & Best debenture timber & make the rest of the Load with long small Pieces. the large timber shoud not be left than 20 feet in length the S. Valley maidens have stoln a piece of Whim Rope to day they are to be discharg'd to morrow unless they will Confess who stole it how did you get on at W Abram Sale to day Did you buy any thing. is the lode Cut in the X cut yet. Cap tn Rule Jr will go down to morrow on thursday

WPe Sherick

The Day and Night Book– 26 August 1823

24 Septr 1823

Captn James

I want to have the dial which you
have at Bolenoe with the level in it to dial
the 4.2 X Cut North ♯ the 70 west ✗ the a dit
End East of R.B. & the X Cut North Captn Kule
wishes me to dial them to marrow so that I shall
want it in the morning I suppose you can
send it down by Jan Pascoe & Davey Thomas
Captn Kule wishes you & Captn Harry to get Captn
Tilbert & Robin to spend more money than they
will receive go to dinner with them if possible
& Order 2 or 3 Bottle of wine & make them
pay their Part & If Captn Harry can find any
old Coal woman with her Cowal to Dog them
around the street t'would be glorious fun
for I think we shall want something or other
to keep our spirits up on Saturday next by what
I can see of it. to marrow I shall measure
at Central & H. Broaze & on Friday go to W Francis
& to B. Wood account on Saturday we ought to be
here in pretty good Season

Wm P Menick

The Day and Night Book– 24 September 1823

BOLENOWE MINE

Between April and October 1823 a major concern of Captain Thomas was Bolenowe Mine. Despite his heavy commitments in so many different directions, he happily and enthusiastically, took on the management of the newly re-opened Bolenowe Mine.

The first mention of Bolenowe Mine in the journal was on April 25 when Thomas invited two Dolcoath mine captains to the mine, presumably for their opinions and advice. He wrote to Petherick: *Come up to Bolenowe about 11 or 12 o'clock if you can & if you can see Capt Tregoning, ask him to come up with you.* Bolenowe Mine had been abandoned for some time when Thomas took the lease of the sett from Squire Pendarves. Ancient workings to the west of Bolenowe, stretching across the hillside on the south side of Troon, were probably connected to the mine, which was re-opened by Captain Thomas, in 1823. Thomas' first task was to form a group of adventurers, to share the burden of cost for the new project. Up to a dozen adventurers are mentioned in the text: James Thomas, William Petherick, William Rule, Joseph Rule, Richard Rule, Charles Thomas, C. Harvey, J. Harvey, John Phillips, Mr Drake and the Reverend Shallcross. A Mr A. Penrose was also mentioned as an adventurer, who sold his share to a Londoner, but Thomas might have been referring to Dolcoath and not Bolenowe. Others may have included Captain Rule senior, and the two mine captains who inspected the mine, Tregoning and Skinner. At least four of the named adventurers were Dolcoath mine captains, and John Phillips was assayer and bookkeeper at Dolcoath. Charles Thomas was James' older brother, and the three Rules were cousins of William Petherick. The Harveys and Messers Drake and Shallcross appear to have been later recruits to the adventure, as the context in which they are mentioned suggests Thomas 'selling' the scheme to them.

It was common practice among mine managers to seek the opinions of external experts. The reference above to captains Tregoning and Petherick being asked to visit the newly opened mine was typical. On July 30 Captain Skinner of West Wheal Wellington, another newly re-opened mine, inspected Bolenowe Mine for Thomas, and undoubtedly shared his thoughts on its prospects. Captain Rule, manager of Dolcoath, also advised on appropriate engines for the mine, as did Dolcoath's engineer, James Gribble. The Camborne community was always supportive of new schemes to expand mining in the area, and despite local rivalries, tended to encourage and help their neighbours.

By July 4 1823 Captain Thomas was arranging what appears to have been the first meeting of the adventurers of Bolenowe Mine. Thomas told Petherick that he was to call on Mr Pendarves that morning to fix a date for a meeting of the adventurers. On the night of July 16, Thomas said: *The resolution signed at the meeting was to colect £5 per share – but I shall colect only 50/- from all those that I colected last time. If you will be so good as to speak to Messers Joseph & W'm Rule to that effect, and if I could have the money on Saturday, I shall feel much obliged. Try to see Mr Philips too. I have spoken to Charles. I must try to get the money to pay the men on Saturday afternoon.* What the total number of shares was we do not know, nor how many adventurers were involved, so we cannot know how big the project was, but £5 a share was not a small amount for the modest adventurers whose names we know.

How many men worked at Bolenowe we do not know. Only four possible names of miners employed there were mentioned in the Day & Night Book: Dick Trezona, W. Daniel, Davy Thomas and Stephen Vine. All of them were ostensibly employed at Dolcoath Mine, and it appears that James Thomas may have seconded them quietly and unofficially, for a spot of moonlighting at his pet project. On the night of May 26 1823 Petherick asked Thomas somewhat irritably: *Does Dick Trezona work at Bolenoe. He has not been working but one core in the end!* Thomas replied: *Trezona's end is hard & ugly. I asked them about Dick – he has been up a few stems with W Daniel – at South Bolenowe.* A suspicious Petherick asked the following night: *Did you know of Dick Trezona's being at South Bolenoe? They kept it a most wonderful secret from me, indeed if I had not discovered it for myself, & that too quite by accident, perhaps I shoul'd never have known it. If Dick has not your consent to go he never had mine, & I think if that is the case, he must have our consent to stay away. I do not like such little mean tricks at all, and that Dick is a first rate shaver* (Glossary), *is as notorious as the sun at noon day. But enough of Dick & all such scamps.* One of the miners at Bolenowe was Davy Thomas. It seems that Captain Thomas sought, unsuccessfully, to divert Petherick's attention away from seconding Dick Trezona to his mine, by telling the younger captain about a wonderful dream Davy Thomas had had: *I am going home to see what is the best news of Bolenowe Mine – Davy Thomas dreamt of a fine course of ore & tin there.* The news had the opposite affect upon Petherick, and he replied with heavy sarcasm about reliance on such things as dreams, before renewing his demand for information from Thomas on the whereabouts of Dick Trezona. On June 3 Thomas sought to explain his attempts to get miners seconded to Bolenowe from Dolcoath: *Steph.Vine was saying he took a pitch at Entral. I called on him this evening as I wanted a man at Bolenowe and he told me he would go, only for me to speake to you about it.* The truth was gradually being revealed to the younger captain. By the end of June Petherick seems to have accepted his colleagues questionable recruitment regime and was asking him how he had got on with the *setting at Bolenowe?* Presumably, with the mine moving to a regular footing, miners were being given proper contracts, to open up the mine. This is confirmed by the entry for the following day, when Thomas wrote: *I have taken the liberty of taking your dial. I want to use it at Bolenowe Mine a few hours.* It was to prove a long *few hours*, for three months later Petherick demanded the return of the instrument: *I want to have the dial which you have at Bolenowe with the level in it to dial the 42 Xcut north, the 70 west ...* The particular instrument borrowed was not the average dial used underground at that time, but one with a level in it, enabling Captain Thomas to level the adit and workings rather than just determine directions.

When work began at Bolenowe Mine the existing infrastructure included the old engine shaft and adit system. The fixed plant also, apparently, included an old water engine, which although probably adequate for the original workings, was insufficient for the needs of the new mine envisaged by Thomas. On July 9 Petherick asked Thomas: *How do you get on forking the water at Bolenowe? Will it be all in fork on Friday morning? If it should be, I think I'll run down to see the lode & perhaps Cousin W'm will go down too.* The next day Thomas replied: *I am going home to see how they come on under the adit. I saw them last night & this morning* (the) *water* (was) *in fork ... I believe the water will be too much for men to keep.* Clearly, despite the waterwheel powered engine getting the water out to below the adit level, Thomas did not believe it would be powerful enough to cope when the mine deepened, and four days later, on July 14, Petherick referred to Thomas' plan to obtain a steam engine to drain the mine. *Capt Rule was saying to me today that he thought Jas.Gribble, Engineer, would approve of that cylinder at R(oskear) B(roase) for Bolenowe.* That night Thomas said he intended to speak to Gribble about the Roskear Broase cylinder, but two days later another engine was being spoken of. Petherick wrote (July 16): *How much does Mr Williams ask for his Engine? Will it come cheaper than Jemmy Gribbles?* Captain Thomas replied: *I am going with Mr Gribble to see Mr Williams Engine. We shall see whether it is compleat & good or not and know the price, etc. If we can have a little Engine second hand cheap, it will be exactly the thing we want.* After examining Williams' engine it appears that Gribble advised to stick with the one he had. On July 21 Thomas reported: *I have been with Mr Gribble today examining R(oskear) Broase cylinder, etc, with the nozells at W(heal) Bryant, etc. I spoke to Capt Rule about them and he says that we shall have them in a moderate price – so I told him I would take them, as Capt Joe from S(outh) Roskear was waiting to accept if I refused. I think we should get an Engine cheap in this way.* On the night of the 24th Petherick wrote: *I suppose you've been very busy today, as I see the cylinder heav'd out.* Clearly, Captain Thomas did not want to waste any time. Six weeks later, on September 8, Thomas attended a mine sale at Penberthy Crofts, and purchased a *few fms of Rods and some oak for lentells for Engine house.* The Cornish steam pumping engine, its house and the pitwork in the engine shaft were all coming together.

The most important part of a successful copper mine is the lode. The quality and quantity of copper or tin ore was the most significant factor in determining whether the mine was to be successful. Captain James Thomas' optimism might have been bolstered by Davy Thomas' dream, but Petherick needed more practical reassurance, based upon scientific examination and assay. As noted above, as soon as the water was forked he and William Rule, would *run down to see the lode.* The following day Thomas commented, that the miners had *brought up some of the South part of the lode, which made a good van … I'll try to ascertain the size and quality of the lode.* Three weeks later (July 30) Captain Skinner visited Bolenowe Mine, to get his own view of its lode and prospects. Things must have looked good, because a week later Captain Thomas was at Penberthy

Crofts buying gear for the new mine. Even Petherick was in optimistic mood when he told Thomas, on September 17: *As soon as Bolenowe is cut rich, J Phillips, R'd Rule and myself are going to Scilly, Dublin, Paris, Cadiz, Pisa & the Isle of Scio & where also I don't know as yet.* A week later Captain Thomas sent a sample for Phillips to assay, believing that it might contain copper. Thomas described the location and appearance of the lode it came from. *It came from Bolenowe, not from the + cut south, but from the Engine Shaft ... there appears to be a lode coming in the shaft from the north, fine gossan peach & mundic &, I hope, copper ... if there is any copper in it, it will be worth something* Regrettably, the sample did not contain copper, much to the adventurers' disappointment. Petherick was back to his sarcastic self about the value of the mine, when commenting on a visit by two prospective investors, on October 16: *Be sure you don't cut a course of ore against Mr Drake & Shallcross ... because they would be so much affronted as to run away.* Apparently, the lode had still not proved valuable and the young mine captain's confidence remained lower than his enthusiastic older colleague.

We know something of Bolenowe Mine from other sources. The adit to which Captain Thomas referred, was called *Mr Pollard's adit*, in John Coster's *Observations on Sundry Mines* (mid-18th century CRO), and the portal exhausted into the stream at Bolenowe Croft. (SW 673/383) The fall from the centre of the mine (SW 669/382) was some 117 feet (35m), which would probably mean that the adit came into the workings at Engine Shaft about 100 feet below surface. According to the *Royal Cornwall Gazette* of January 31 & April 3 1824, and the *West Briton* of July 27 1827, a 24-inch steam engine, with a 3½ ton iron beam, was erected on the mine and was pumping by April 1824. The engine was advertised for sale in July 1827. It was stated that the workings were sunk to a depth of twelve fathoms in 1824, but this does not agree with what we know of the workings when Captain Thomas re-started the mine. The report probably meant 12 fathoms below adit, which was at least 16 fathoms deep. The lode being opened up by Thomas, was known as Bolenowe North Lode, and was only a few inches wide, but was very rich in tin. In the 1840s and 1860s Great Gossan Lode and South Lode, which lay to the south of Thomas' mine, were explored. (AKHJ vol.10. p.50) In the 1860s captains Thomas and Tonkin of Dolcoath both wrote reports on the lode at Bolenowe, including the one worked by James Thomas in the 1820s.

THE MINE AT SURFACE

Although captains Petherick and Thomas were primarily concerned with the underground workings at the Valley Section of Dolcoath, there are numerous references to what lay at surface. The mine offices were known as the Accompt or Account House, and are generally now referred to as Count Houses. Most large mines had two or more Account Houses, to serve the needs of the miners and mine captains in the widely spread sections of the mine. On the night of January 2 1823 Captain Thomas referred to the *south acc't house*. Where this was situated cannot easily be determined, but it is likely that it served the western end of the mine, as these workings lay further south than those at Bullen Garden and the Valley. In the same entry Thomas mentioned the *material house*, or stores, which the mine captains also used for socialising. He met Captain Robin there and shared *a drop of gin … a little toddy*. Thomas tells Petherick that he will find some brandy there also, *which may serve to comfort your heart after you come up from underground*. Thomas mentioned a bedroom in the material house, which suggests that the day and night captains could sleep there when on call but not underground.

On January 10 Captain Thomas spoke of the *Rolling mill flores*, where 120 tons of copper ore were to be crushed. On April 11 Petherick mentioned them: *The parcel on the North floor will be about 105, produce 6½, on the South floor, 50, produce 13. Rolling mill floors, stampt ores 120, produce 10/- . In all 275 tons = produce price £6. Amount £1650*. Cornish Rolls or Copper Rolls were invented, or at least introduced into Cornwall and Devon, by John Taylor at Wheal Crowndale, on the Tamar, and Consolidated Mines, in Gwennap. The rollers were water-powered and could quickly crush large tonnages of ore. They represented a huge saving in labour, especially among the bal maidens, but although Dolcoath clearly had at least one such crusher, they were not in universal use at the mine, because the bal maidens continued to carry out their tasks as before. According to Burt (John Taylor 1977) they were first introduced into his Devon mines by Taylor in 1806, but it was 1823 before they were considered efficient, and

1831 before Taylor introduced them into Consolidated at Gwennap. Taylor appears to have learned about them from the North of England where they were already in use. Robert Hunt commented in the 1880s: "From that time to the present, the roller crushing mill has formed the principal apparatus for reducing mixed lead and copper ores." There is some disagreement over whether the rolling mills were used early in the dressing process, to reduce the ore for easy separation, or later in the process, to replace the buckers. There is no record of John Taylor registering a patent for any such machinery. Dolcoath's rolling mills appear to have been situated in the valley, close to the Red River.

As well as the rolling mill floors, the above entry refers to the *North floor* and the *South floor*. These floors were large, flat, cobbled areas on which the ore was broken and sorted for sampling. Ore from particular shafts was carried to designated floors, and then divided according to ownership for processing. The floors themselves were divided into areas to ensure proper ore separation. Petherick's entry for February 15 1823 has: *Our ores will, I believe, make the following mixtures. The stampt ore, about 130 tons, produce 4½, to be divided on the South part of the South floor. 80 tons, produce 6: this takes in all the Valley ores & will be divided on the North floor. 60 tons, produce 9: this mixture will be all the ore brought down from Water Whim (Shaft). I have settled it thus, in consequence of there not being floor room enough on the North floor & 140 tons would be rather too much for one parcel.* This complicated description of where ore from various places was to be sorted, how much there was and what its metal produce was expected to be, indicates the complex surface arrangements for breaking and dressing copper ore in an important section of a large early nineteenth century copper mine. It is also informative on the responsibilities of the underground 'day and night' captain toward tributers' ore, until sampling has been carried out and the miners' share calculated. The fourth copper floors mentioned in the journal were the eastern floors.

On August 14 Captain Thomas wrote: *I should think it proper for the ores on the Eastren floors to be sampl'd there. You may ask Capt Rule's opinion.* As the North and South floors appear to have been in the valley, alongside the Red River, it seems that the eastern floors may well have been on the flat ground close to Water Whim Shaft. The entry for February 15 speaks of Water Whim Shaft ore being *brought down* to North floors. Water Whim or Valley (Eastern) Shaft is high up on the brow of the eastern side of the Red River Valley.

Two parts of the dressing area were referred to by Petherick when he described the apprehension of the bal maidens caught thieving. The April 17 entry mentions *Spargoe's Cobbing House* and *Bartle's picking tables*. Petherick described going into the house where the picking tables were situated, and catching the bal maids there. From this it appears that both the maidens working on the picking tables and those employed cobbing the ore, worked inside houses or buildings. Cobbing involved knocking copper ore from waste rock with a special 'cobbing' hammer. Picking was simply removing unwanted waste rock from previously broken ore. Also mentioned in Petherick's account of the 17th, was the *burninghouse*. The man on duty at the burninghouse was called *little Jack Burninghouse*, and he assisted Petherick to pursue the girls and cause them to drop their loot.

The burninghouse was a cause of some irritation to the mine captains. On the night of February 20 1823 Captain Petherick moaned: *O the infernal Burning House smoke. I'm almost chok'd with it.* Seven months later, on the night of September 30 he again complained about it: *I've been almost chok'd with the poison tonight. It's as dark as a pit & most dreadfull flood of rain. I expect to be white against I get home.* Most burninghouses in use at the time were not intended to produce arsenic as a by-product, so much as burn off arsenic and sulphides from tin. Although arsenic was being produced in Cornwall by the early nineteenth century, there is no evidence that Dolcoath produced or sold any as early as 1823. The poisonous fumes and smoke were discharged into the atmosphere, frequently to the detriment of local people, livestock and land. In 1828 William Brunton patented his machinery for calcining ore in order to extract arsenic soot for sale, and this calciner was to become the mostly widely used for the purpose in nineteenth and twentieth century Cornwall.

Other references to the burninghouse in the journal show it to have had an important role in tin production at Dolcoath. On February 6 1823 Petherick asked Thomas to send *one of the Burning House boys down to me tomorrow with the dressing cost book*, and on April 2 he asked Thomas to *send down the little Vincent from the Burning House tomorrow* for the same purpose. This suggests that several youngsters were employed assisting the men who operated the burninghouse. On August 4 and 5 the burninghouse was at the centre of activity as the mine increased tin output. Thomas wrote: *I have been with Capt Rule today looking at Tin Stuff, Burning House, Fire Stamps, etc, etc*. Petherick replied: *No drawing tonight. All hands have been working at the Burninghouse about the tin*. It seems probable that the burninghouse lay in the valley beside the Red River. The map of the Camborne and Illogan Mining District, by Robert Symons, dated 1850, shows a calciner near to the river, close to North Valley Shaft. Almost certainly, this occupied the spot where the offending burninghouse once stood.

The fire stamps mentioned were also part of the tin production side of the mine, and during 1823 the white metal became increasingly important to what was principally a copper mine. On March 17 1823 Petherick reported: *Busily employ'd all this night at fire stamps. Tell Capt Robin, if you see him tomorrow, that he must give our 3 smiths a stem each for assisting to get the axle in its place*. Petherick was less impressed by the maintenance smiths, on the night of June 9, when he wrote: *The fire stamps has been idle untill 11 o'clock & no smith to be found to make a cutter. Spale the bugger 20s*. As always, maintenance men go quickly from hero to villain on a mine: praised for working all night in March and condemned for being tucked up in bed in June.

Like most mines which produced tin, Dolcoath also employed water-powered stamps. These machines, first referred to in Cornwall in the 1490s, in Wendron, were to be found in almost every valley in west Cornwall. The Red River had sets of water stamps between Bolenowe and the sea at Gwithian from the sixteenth century onwards. The 1737 map of Tehidy Manor, drawn by William Doidge, shows such stamps all along the valley between Brea Village and Tuckingmill. Remnants of these water stamps can still be found there, and the leats which fed them can still be traced without difficulty. It is surprising, given their ubiquitousness, that only one mention is made of these stamps in the Day & Night Book. James Thomas visited the *red river stamps* with Captain Robin on May 13 1823.

Throughout the journal there are references to whims, mostly to do with breakages and other problems. On April 20 1823 there was a specific reference to a *horse whim*. These ubiquitous machines were moved around all the mines of the period, being easily dismantled and re-erected.

FOOD & DRINK

One subject which appears on over fifty pages of the journal is food and drink. No subject seemed to fill the conversation of these two miners quite like their constant interest in what there was to eat, where they had eaten and what they had drunk. Surprisingly, these references are extremely informative on a range of matters. They tell us what sort of food was available, how different types of meat were graded, what alcoholic drinks were available on the mine, who the suppliers were, and what a typical hotel or inn might have on the menu.

The subject was introduced at the very beginning of the journal, in Petherick's dedication, to: *Our Noble selves, Knights of the most Honourable order of Beef Stews & Steaks. Knights Companions of the Roast Goose & Generals of the Morning Rashers.* When Captain Thomas came up from underground on December 11 1822, after describing his examination of the south lodes and problems at the 100 and 110fm levels at Water Whim Shaft, and telling his colleague that he wanted to be home early the following day to turn over his garden before the frosts set in, he wrote: *There's a bit of fresh pork for a steak for supper, and some salt pork for breakfast, so you will not want meat.* Apart from fresh pork and salted pork, the two captains mention boiled pork and stinking pork, which was clearly not fit to eat. Goose was also a favourite meat, and they had both wings and legs roasted. Ham was regularly on the menu, as was tongue, veal cutlets, beef, both roasted and stewed, bacon rashers, mutton, herring, chicken and hare pie. Christmas 1822 saw them enjoying *ale & cakes* with the management, presumably in the Account House. There are frequent mentions of boiled eggs, kept *in the desk*, and bread and cheese. Not only did Petherick and Thomas have breakfast when they came up from underground, but they also occasionally carried a piece of ham or other meat in their pockets to chew on whilst climbing through the workings.

On June 18 1823 William Petherick went to Penzance to sell some of

Dolcoath's tin. After the business was done he went for dinner at the Union Hotel, in Chapel Street. *I took dinner at the Union Hotel, Penzance; veal cutlet with egg sauce, gooseberry & jelly tarts, new potatoes, strawberries & cherries of a very superior kind. Din'd alone. Strawberries & cream are very good.* On September 3 James Thomas was able compete with his colleague on the quality of his dinner: *Din'd at Fosses Hotel yesterday, on roast beef, mutton, goose, pies, puddings, wine, punch etc, etc.* Perhaps the dainty fare available at the Union Hotel in Penzance was not on the menu at Fosses Hotel, Redruth, but Thomas certainly enjoyed a wide variety of meats there. A trip to Penzance would have been an outing for these men, but Redruth was regularly visited by them, and Fosses Hotel was the venue for the Masonic lodge to which James Thomas belonged. Unfortunately, the place where Thomas, Robin and Jilbert dined in Truro on September 25, when the latter two were subject to 'wind up' by the other captains, is not named in the journal, and nor is the menu. All we know is that several bottles of wine were to be consumed.

Alcoholic drink was frequently mentioned by both mine captains in the journal. Ale, brandy, gin (grog), punch and wine were regularly consumed and enjoyed by them. James Thomas, the Wesleyan class leader and local preacher was as keen as the next man on each of those beverages, and William Petherick rarely missed a chance for a drink. After work, alcohol was advocated to restore the spirits, and when miners were involved in an accident or had a 'near miss', alcohol was suggested to help them get over it. It was recommended both as a restorative and as a source of pleasure. Captains Thomas and Petherick were men of their class and background and viewed alcohol in the same way as their fellow miners.

The principal suppliers of food and drink to the mine were Mr and Mrs Knapp, of Knapp's Hotel, in Camborne. Knapp's Hotel appears to have been located on Fore Street Camborne, the principal street in the town (information from David Thomas). There were regular references to obtaining and paying for food and alcohol from the Knapps, who were not only small-time adventurers in local mines, but also friends of the two mine captains. William Petherick was godfather to one of the Knapp children.

CONCLUSION

There are many features of this journal which might surprise those familiar with the popular picture of early 19th century miners. The devout Wesleyan local preacher, Captain James Thomas, was a Freemason; women, not men, were the most numerous attendees at Cornish miners' funerals; alongside the deeply held Christian convictions of many of those miners was a deep-rooted fatalism; strong liquor was as popular with the Methodist preacher as it was with the roughest miner, and strong and often obscene language was used as much by the chapel-goer as by those less-inclined to attend places of worship.

There is a widely held view that Methodism and Freemasonry do not mix. That may well be the case now, but it certainly was not so during the 19th century. When Cornish miners went to the American, South African or Australian mining towns they needed contacts to find work and get on. Joining the local Masonic lodge in Redruth, St Day or Camborne was a successful net-working strategy. Upon arriving in Butte, Grass Valley, Bendigo or Ballarat the newly arrived miner would register at the local lodge, giving his home lodge and his number. Membership of the local Methodist chapel was another help in establishing himself in his new country. Captain James Thomas, a Wesleyan local preacher, was a member of Redruth Druids Lodge, which met at Fosse's Hotel.

Until relatively recently, many Cornish funerals were attended only by men. Even in the late 20th century some miners' funerals had no women in attendance, other than possibly the widow and a couple of close female relatives. Many believe that the 'all male funeral' was a Cornish tradition, but the comment by Captain William Petherick on those who went to the funeral of F. Bartle, on January 9 1823, shows that in the 1820s the opposite was the case. An *immense concourse of people present & I believe 2 or 3 females to 1 male according to custom.*

A characteristic of Cornish miners and bal maids which shines through everything written in this Day & Night Book, was their independence. Bal maids disputed with their bosses over their pay, without being intimidated. Bal maidens caught thieving defied the mine officials without fear, and when they were fired they did not hesitate to go the other end of the mine and get taken on again. They fought their corner and argued their case with little deference or regard for the possible consequences. Miners were rarely overawed by the mine captains and gave as good as they got when there was a dispute over a pitch, or a price or any other area of disagreement. The mine captains were likewise outspoken when they needed to make a point to the manager or the agents of the copper companies.

The Cornish miners' sense of humour is irrepressible. Thomas Beare, who described the miners and tin streamers of the 16th century, gave many examples of their humour, which was often outrageous and sometimes verged on the obscene. Captains Thomas and Petherick found much to amuse them in their daily work, and never missed a chance to relate some funny incident, joke or wind-up. The aged mine manager, Captain John Rule, although well into his 70s, not only enjoyed a laugh himself, but was involved in planning a most carefully orchestrated wind-up of two of his old mine captains. How he must have laughed as his nephew, William Petherick told of Captains Jilbert and Robin being forced to pay for wine they could not afford and then being dogged around the streets of Truro by an old woman carrying a coal basket. The fun the mine captains and bal maidens had at the expense of the copper agents was also described in some detail.

The beliefs of these two men may well have been typical of men of their background and time. In some ways they stood at opposite ends of the Camborne Wesleyan spectrum. One was a Wesleyan local preacher who was fired with a great zeal for his Lord. He was devout, kind, generous and sympathetic toward the poor miners he was responsible for and for his poorer neighbours who had less materially than he and his family did. Throughout the journal his tolerance of weakness and kindness toward the hard-working miners shone through. John Harris, the miner poet, whose family were neighbours to the Thomases at Bolenowe, told in his autobiography of how Captain James Thomas threw open his library to him. Undoubtedly, when the young poet joined his father underground at

Dolcoath, James Thomas would have kept an eye out for him. Captain William Petherick, on the other hand, was less devout although just as interested in religious questions. He waxed eloquent over the ransom sacrifice of Jesus Christ, although he thought that those who were paid for it should be the ones to explain it. Like Thomas he attended chapel and even went to hear preachers outside the usual Sunday services. Unlike the older man, Petherick was not superstitious and was quite scathing about such things as 'dream lodes'. He was also less sympathetic toward those he thought were deviating from strict honesty in their dealings with the mine. Thieves should be fired; negligent or careless miners should not be able to claim off the Club if they suffered due to their own actions; malingerers should be disciplined and those who tried to fiddle their hours should be dismissed.

A characteristic, which has helped the Cornish miner cope with the dangers inherent in his daily work, has been a certain fatalism. Methodism taught the Cornish that by accepting Jesus Christ they were saved, and that once this temporary struggle was over, eternity in heaven awaited them. Similarly, fatalism gave the miner reassurance, by teaching him not to worry unduly about the dangers he faced, because if it was his time, there was nothing he could do about it. When your number is up, it's up! This also comes over in the journal, especially when Captain Thomas spoke of the unfortunate death of Ned George: *I am very sorry to hear of the misfortune that has happen'd to Ned George – poor old fellow his dowsen is all over ... but its appointed for men once to die.*

The modern Methodist view of strong liquor is also at odds with the attitudes of these two men and their Wesleyan friends. Throughout the journal there are mentions of alcohol being consumed by them both. Gin and wine were seen as legitimate sources of support and pleasure. They enjoyed their grog – 'Holland Gin' – wine and any other strong drink available to them. The temperance movement had not yet taken off in Camborne, as it was to, dividing congregations and splitting many a devout Wesleyan family.

It is important to see these two men as 'of their time'. They were both from families which had worked hard and were lifting themselves out of the poverty of most of their working-class neighbours. As mine captains they were on the ladder upwards. Their background was similar to that of their neighbours, as was their education. They were both used to hard physical work, as were the men they were responsible for and the bosses they were answerable to. Everyone involved in the mining industry, indeed everyone employed in every industry in the 19th century, worked hard for long periods with little rest and few breaks. For most men and women the words holiday or vacation had little meaning. Even many marriages took place on Boxing Day or some other time when work ceased for a day or two.

The unselfconscious nature of what was written by these two men, make the entries in this journal priceless. There was no attempt to impress an outside readership, or colour the public perception of miners and bal maidens. It was, for the two authors, a straightforward description of what they had done that day or night, with gossip as it had been heard, together with suggestions on what they thought should be done in any one of a hundred situations. Thus, there is no 'side' to the journal – it was merely two hard-working tired men having a private chat about work, life and the universe. Nothing is censured, nothing is left out for the sake of diplomacy, opinions were honestly and freely expressed. When offence was given the offender tended to shrug it off and the offended one just got on with it, as friends do. The picture it paints of life in an important Cornish copper mine in the 1820s is probably unique. The insight gained from these two remarkable but typical Cornish miners, is incomparable.

THE MINERS

Henry Abram (Abraham) Henry Abram was a tributer who also carried out occasional tutwork and stent work on the owners account. In August 1823 he and his partners had launders sent down to the 40fm level and ladders sent to the 50fm level. The launders carried water on the 40 level and the ladders were for a ladder road below the 50fm level. They looked for payment for these tasks to be added either to their tribute contract or to be paid on piece work rates.

Michael Abram (Abraham) He was a tributer. We have no information as to where he worked, but in March 1823 his pitch was failing and the mine captain suggested he give it another month and try to get enough ore for sampling.

Peter Abram (Abraham) Peter and W. Abram were tributers. In May 1823 they did some timbering and in July through to September they were referred to as working in Valley Section. On July 11 Abram requested that his ore be sampled with that from the pitches of William Jenkins, Thomas Spargoe and John Vincent, rather than with the Valley ore. On August 5 Captain Thomas wrote that Peter and his pare had a *bunch* of ore 3ft high by 1ft wide, but three days later the mine captain reported that the ore was failing.

W. Abram (Abraham) Worked with Peter Abram (above).

(?) Abram (Abraham) This Abram is never given a Christian name in the journal. He was the senior timberman or binder and he is referred to throughout the Day & Night Book, possibly more frequently than any other miner. Up to forty entries in the journal mention him. Most of the references have him working with one Crase, who appears to have been his right-hand man. They were most frequently concerned with keeping shafts open and safe, and sometimes this involved carrying out highly dangerous work. To inspect and repair the shaft timbering they used a 'couch' which appears to have been a sort of suspended platform or plank on which the timbermen sat as they were lowered down the shafts to carry out their tasks. On March 2 1823 it was reported that whilst thus engaged a rock had fallen from the side of the shaft and *bravely frightened* Abram, who, it was suggested, would feel better after a stiff drink. On 23 April Captain Petherick accompanied Abram on the 'couth' for an inspection of North Valley Shaft, possibly to give moral support to the previously frightened timberman, but in June Abram and his pare had another near miss while on the 'couch', and again they were severely shaken by it. Abram and Crase continued working in the shafts but Abram was clearly worried by the incidents, and a month later Petherick asks Thomas after Abram's health and asks if he was fit for work? *Shou'd he have the fear I shou'd be very sorry for him.* Within days, however, Abram and Crase were back in their routine, inspecting and repairing the shafts. On July 30 they sorted out the timber in South Valley Shaft, which had been causing the kibbles to catch, a week later they installed a new ladder road and on August 7 they were involved in a major problem with Machine Shaft. A large amount of rock had fallen into the shaft from above the 60fm level, and apparently choked the shaft for a depth of eight to ten fathoms above the 134fm level. Petherick reckoned solving the problem was going to be long, expensive and dangerous, and that Abram was the best man for the task. The situation was so serious that the following day Captain Rule, the manager became involved. Thomas wrote to Petherick: *Abram is to be sent down from the 40 (Machine) thro' the shaft tomorrow, to see what state the ground is in over the 60. I have held a counsell with Capn Rule etc about the job. If Abram thinks it will stand for a few months we may be better able to repair it – but if its in danger of falling away we must try to secure it. Richard Pryors men & John Jenkin with 2 of Adam's will do to assist Abram about it.* Thomas also arranged for the tributers whose pitches were endangered by the unstable ground to put in stull pieces to protect their backs above the 134fm level at Valley Shaft. They were also to *put back all the attle that is in the machine shaft, which is about 10fms in height* – £6 6s. Machine and North Valley shafts were adjacent to each other.

Abram and Crase also carried out repairs in the other shafts in Valley Section, including work in South Valley Shaft and Gossan Shaft. They were also responsible for maintaining the adit system, and in September

1823 they were paid 2s 6d a stem each for going into the Deep Adit, which had been neglected by Cooks Kitchen adit men.

Abram's job gave him opportunities to fiddle and charge twice for timber. Petherick accused him of this in May 1823: *If I'm not mistaken we have paid for that same identical timber 2 or 3 times already. I suppose it's a plan between them together to raise a pint.* The next day Petherick humbly apologised for his *writing to you perhaps a little angrily on the subject*, but explained that he still thought it all rather suspicious.

Abram had a certain wayward reputation with women. Several comments show him to have had a wandering eye, and after a particularly difficult job, he requested that apart from his wages he required *three weeks round among the women after he has finished.* Captain Thomas replied to this: *Be so good as to tell Abram that I think one week, instead of three will do for him – as Sheaby is still able to work & talk – and she has said that if ever she knows Abram to go with any other women she will put hot lead on his ear.*

Henry Adams He could have been either a tutworker or tributer as the mentions of him do not make it clear. When Machine Shaft was choked with attle in August 1823 he appears to have been working between the 40 and 60fm levels as it was suggested that two of his men assist Abram in repairing the shaft there. Adams was involved in a dispute over Tom Spargoe's alleged promise to take young Nicky Richards onto his contract for a week. It appears possible that Nicky normally worked with Adams, who had nothing for him to do for a week.

(?) **Allen** Allen appears to have been a tributer working on the 145fm level near to Gossan Shaft. In October 1823 the shaft was damaged at the 90fm level, and Allen and his pare needed Abram to repair it so that they could send their ore kibbles to surface.

James Bennetts Bennetts could have been either a tributer or a tutworker. In January 1823 the journal records that his 'charges' had been settled, on March 17th he and his partners were kibble filling on night shift, and in June he was severely injured whilst climbing down a ladder road. Three 'staves' or rungs were missing on the second ladder above the 80fm level, and Bennetts sprained his side, being then forced to climb over 600 feet back to surface. There was almost certainly another James Bennetts in Valley section as the mine captain used Bennetts' nickname of 'Patience', when reporting the accident.

John Bennetts He was a tributer. It appears that he had both tin and copper in the pitch he was working on July 21 1823. A week later Thomas Rogers & partners sought permission to work *John Bennetts's Old Pitch.* Petherick thought them *pretty good hands for such a place & if you've no objection we'll sett it to them.* By 'such a place' Petherick might have referred to the fact that there was tin ore with the copper there. A couple of references to Bennetts being paid for timbering might indicate that the stope where he worked was in need of extra support, or it might have referred to the routine installation of stulls for attle.

Uncle Jacky Benner He appears to have been a timberman who carried out routine support work, installed ladders and did general underground labouring. Benner was paid by stem (day pay) on the 'owners' account'. He appears to have been something of a character, with a sense of humour, who liked to 'wind up' the younger mine captain. On July 2 1823 Petherick wrote: *Uncle Jacky Benner & ptrs have been here & only asked the moderate sum of £20 for the job. I told them we shou'd not give any such money nor nothing like it if the shaft was never repaired. This week is enough for the job & they are but three of them, Abram to assist. What say you to giving them £9 & 20/- to Abram – I think it is money enough.* Predictably, the following day, Petherick commented: *Uncle Jack Benner & pare look rather chuff at the price – I told them we wou'd give no more.* During July there were several references to captains Thomas and Petherick negotiating with Benner over payments for a variety of jobs, including clearing a winze between the 118 and 125fm levels and putting in a footway (ladder road) and doing maintenance work in North Valley Shaft. Like Abram, Benner appears to have been a lady's man, and in June 1823 he was boasting about his latest conquest. *Uncle Jack was swaggering that he had a smart lady yesterday – Abram & Crase can tell you all the story – he was up all night with her etc etc etc.*

(?) Crase Like his partner, Abram, Crase was never given a Chistian name. Every references to him is in association with Abram, the senior timberman.

Young Crase He was a tributer. The only mention of him is interesting. Petherick wrote: *The Young Crase has been here tonight to know whether we had any objections to his giving up his pitch or not. I told he might go when he pleas'd & where he pleas'd, so he departed very well pleas'd & in so doing I pleas'd myself & hope I've pleas'd you, if so we shall be pleas'd altogether.* Perhaps Young Crase was not up to the job and Captain Petherick was glad to see the back of him.

Old Tom Crase It seems likely that Old Tom was a retired miner. The only reference to him is from September 8 1823, when he stormed into the mine and demanded to know why Petherick had not let his son work with Oppy & pare. He shouted and swore and said he would see the manager and the purser about it.

William Crase William appears to have been the son of Old Tom Crase. On March 12 Petherick said: *I saw James Oppy today & a man with him of the name Jefferey, who wishes to go in William Crase's place.* Whether William had been ill or injured when Oppy had replaced him in his 'pare', we cannot know. Perhaps when William was recovered he sought to return to his old job and had been turned away, causing the old man to demand his reinstatement with Oppy.

Henry Davey He was a tributer working on one of the Entral lodes. On June 3 1823 he was paid 25/- for work done to take up the water and put in a ladder at Water Stile Shaft. He complained that it was not enough, and Thomas suggested he see Petherick and he might get a few shillings more. On the 12th Petherick commented that *Henry Davey will do very well on his ore notwithstanding his growls & grumbles.* Ten days later Thomas visited Davey's pitch and noted that there was plenty of mundic and some good copper ore. Three weeks later Petherick went to the pitch and saw an estimated 20 tons of ore there.

Tom Davis On the night of October 6 1823 *Tom Davis & ptrs* were cleaning the 80fm level west of Water Whim Shaft, under the direction of James Pascoe. It seems probable that he was either a tutworker or tributer, who was doing temporary work on the 'owners' account'.

Henry Dennis He was a tributer. On August 1 1823 there was a *run in Dennis's pitch – it has been a nice chance for them*. The run of ground had obviously filled their pitch with broken ore, which they could separate and send to surface. Four days later Dennis and his 'pare' were given John Viall's pitch, which they could start once they had cleared the ore from their old pitch.

(?) Donithorne No Christian name is given and only one reference is found for him. On July 9 1823 Captain Thomas wrote: *I have been to R (oskear) Broase today and Donithorne went round to soundey – I think we shall get thro' soon*. The 'soundey' mentioned is sounding the rock where the miners expect to break through, in this case into Roskear Broase Shaft.

(?) George The only reference to this man was on January 14 1823 by Captain Petherick: *I've been down to R (oskear) Broaze today & found George & Stephen filling the kibble & the boy caulking the cistern, of course the shaft was idle & one core I think they still throw away every day, for they ought get a boy able to fill 3 or 4 kibbles as there are easily enough. George said if that is the case the boy shall fill the kibble tomorrow ...* There appears to have been a problem with the size of the kibbles, the kibble fillers and the landers at Roskear Broaze Shaft, for several times in the previous days there were references to inadequacies in the work of these people at that shaft, and the need for larger kibbles.

(?) Goldby He was a tributer who worked a pitch near to Jenkins' pitch at the 110fm level. In March 1823 Captain Thomas visited the stope and said both pitches were poor.

William Goldsworthy He was a tributer with a reputation for being a *quiet worker*. In April 1823 Goldsworthy & pare lost the pitch they had been working to Spargoe & ptrs, probably being undercut in the Dutch auction on survey day. They were not happy, although Petherick said he thought they might have learned a useful lesson by the loss – i.e. that they should not bid too high for a pitch. He added that: *I expect you will see them tomorrow about a pitch – they are quiet men & I shall be loath to be without them*. This is an example of men failing to get a pitch on survey day and the mine captains finding them one after the auction. A few days later Petherick reported that Sam Spargoe & ptrs were working *with spirit* in

Goldsworthy's old pitch. A month later he told Thomas that Goldsworthy had been given William Warren's old pitch as recommended by the older captain.

Peter Grangey Grangey was a different type of tributer to Goldsworthy. On September 3 1823 Petherick wrote: *Peter Grangey & Rogers & all the whole tote of them were all turn'd off today by Mr Reynolds for a sett of rogues & vagabonds & the pitch sett anew for 6/10d in the pound.* What their alleged fiddle was we do not know, but Tom Rogers had been in trouble in April, when another accusation against him was taken to the purser, William Reynolds. Perhaps Grangey had got into bad company and adopted questionable tactics to increase the value of their ore.

John Harris This was the father of John Harris, the poet. All the references to Harris in the journal are to either his or his brother's 'club money'. It appears likely that Matthew Harris, who was buried on June 4 1823 at Camborne Church, was killed in an accident at Dolcoath in the previous few days. His brother, John, was also paid 'club money' at the same time, and so it is likely they were both involved in the same accident. John and Matthew lived at Bollenow, near Troon, as did Captain Thomas, with whom the family were friends. In the poet's autobiography, he described his father as a tributer, who could be a taciturn man. Ten years later, in about 1833, the thirteen year old future poet went underground to work with his father, some 200 fathoms below surface.

Young Nicky Richards Hick Whether his surname was Richards or Hick we cannot be certain. It is probable that Hick was a family nickname, as it was common when there were several families with the same surname for them to be known by family nicknames. The custom is still practised in parts of west Cornwall. Nicky was at the centre of a row between miners over an alleged promise to take him onto Tom Spargoe's tribute contract for a week. On August 25th 1823 Petherick said: *I've been down to Entral today … there has been a little noise here today between the Young Nicky Richards Hick & Tom Rogers. Henry Adams tells me that there was an agreement made before you by Thomas Spargoe that he should employ Nicky for a week.* That night Captain Thomas angrily replied: *I heard the agreement made between Tom Spargoe & Henry Adams, Spargoe agreed to take Richards* *for a week and if he do not he is a scoundrel.* Spargoe had already taken on Uncle Jemmy Jenkin *&* the young Jemmy and it is possible he no longer needed an extra hand.

H. Hocking He was an underground labourer employed on the 'owners account'. The single reference to Hocking says that the manager, Captain Rule, had agreed for him to be paid *by the stem.*

James Hockin He was a tutworker who was employed in September 1823 driving South Lode on the 100fm level. On the 11th Petherick went to measure Hockin's end but was rather disappointed with his progress *as its rather likely that the 30/- bargain will last them till next survey day at the rate they are going on.* Two days later the mine captain was even more scathing about James Hockin's efforts: *Capt Rule has been saying this week about driving an end west from eastward at 80fms level on the South Lode that we have on the 100 south of South Valley (Shaft). I think it will take James Hockin all this month to compleat his 30/- bargain – if you see them on Monday give them a good rally – they seem to have no more forecast than a grasshopper which sings in the Springtime, laughs in the Autumn & dies in the Winter.* What Hockin's problems were we do not know, but Captain Petherick was unsympathetic whatever they were.

Tom Trumferey He appears to have been a surface maintenance man. The single mention of him was in connection with the need to repair the 'cage' (the vertical drum) on a horse or steam whim. Problems with the 'cage' were making hoisting ore to the surface difficult.

John Ivey He was a tributer with a pitch on the 110fm level. On December 23 1822 Captain Thomas reported: *I came out thro' 110 Xcut, thro' Iveys & Rogers pitches, very dangerous places.* After Christmas John Ivey and Tom Rogers were given fairly generous payments for stems worked, although the reason is not given. On January 13 Petherick said: *Went to examine the state of the stulls up over them west of Valley Shaft at 110 on North Part & found all the attle from 8 to 10 fms west of the shaft in a sinking state – we quickly decamp'd from there & came back through Iveys pitch on South pitch – crawled in through a small hole & found the attle in the same state, all sinking – retreated as quick as possible from these scenes of danger & arrived in Tom Rogers pitch,* *which is as dangerous as any of them.* In June there was further trouble with poorly supported attle close to North Valley Shaft, and again John Ivey's pitch was the location for it. Petherick believed with so much unstable dirt on either side, the shaft could easily be lost.

James James He was a tributer who did occasional maintenance work. Just before Christmas 1822 a dispute broke out between two groups of tributers concerning the limits of their pitches. On the one side there was John Thomas, Richard Thomas and Stephen Vine and on the other James James and partners. Petherick asked Thomas to try to sort it out. On December 23 Thomas reported: *I have been down today with Vine & Ptrs & James & ptrs and heard a great deal of confused talk – one said it's so, the other 'Thee art a liard etc – but in the end of it I told them we should put the pitches together.* That night Petherick reviewed the argument and thought it highly amusing. *I hope Vine & ptrs & James & ptrs are contented now their pitches are consolidated – if they fall out any more we'll call them the Young Consols as long as they live move & have their being – really it's a laughable affair to see & hear a number of men disputing & all about a thing which they all agree or say is worth nothing.* In March there was another dispute involving James James' pitch, this time over a high grade ore sample allegedly from Jem Oppey's pitch, but which Captain Thomas believed had been stolen from James' pitch. In September Richard Thomas and his men were still working with James, carrying out repair work on a shaft. Thomas reported on the night of September 9: *It has happened tonight that the kibble after been tried 20 or 30 times will not go down to the 100fm levell. Do be so good as tell Dick Thomas or James James & ptrs instead of pretending to repair shafts to go & cut pudding turf, for I think it will suit them much better.* Perhaps shaft repair work should have been left to the experts!

Uncle Stephen Jeffery He was tutworker who, in 1823, was employed mostly on the 100fm level. In May Jeffery and Jem Oppey were engaged in holing through into North Valley Shaft at the 100fm level. On the 12th Captain Thomas met them at surface. *Just after I came up I saw Uncle Stephen Jeffrey. Oppey & ptrs looking very cheerful – they told me they had holed the shaft with a boyer after having bor'd about 5 feet.* Two days later Thomas visited the 100fm level: *I have been down thro' North Valley today … went to the 100, spoke with Uncle Stephen thro' the hole – two of them is on one side &*

two on the other. Once the winze kibble they were using was replaced by a larger whim kibble the miners were able to shift more dirt to surface as they broke through to the shaft and opened it up. Almost a month after the holing there was a serious accident. Thomas wrote: *Uncle Stephen Jeffrey had his head cut in a shocking manner by the Holing Engine. I think so bad a wound as ever I saw, the doctor says he hopes that his scul is not hurt.* Petherick was less sympathetic to Jeffery, commenting that night: *I'm sorry for Uncle Stee to have met with such an accident but from all the accounts which I have been able to collect this evening, it was his own carelessness.* Two days later Thomas said that *Uncle Step. Jeffrey is very bad I am told.* Three months passed and on September 8 1823 Petherick reported: *Uncle Ste. Jeffery has begun to work a little today. I hope he will be able to keep on.* By October 4 Jeffery was back to normal, and able to negotiate with Captain Thomas how he wanted his club money paid. What the Holing Engine was is uncertain, but it was certainly a device for breaking through relatively thin ground between workings.

John Jeffrey He was a tributer. On August 5 Captain Rule sett a pitch to him at 10/- in the pound. Six pitches were sett that day and the entry suggests that there were eight men in each pitch.

(?) Jefferey On March 12 1823 James (Jem) Oppey had a new man assigned to him by Captain Thomas, called Jefferey, *who wishes to go in William Crase's place.*

John Jenkin(s) He was a tributer who apparently had a pitch near to Machine Shaft at about the 60fm level. On the night of August 6 Petherick reported that Jenkin's pitch *is running in,* which may have been related to the *quantity of stuff fell away from over the 60 in Machine Shaft and fill'd it about 8 or 10 fms over 134.* On the 8th Captain Thomas said that John Jenkin and several other tributers were to assist in moving stuff from the shaft and securing the timbering there. A few days later Petherick wrote to Thomas *What's become of John Jenkin I don't know.* Jenkin appears to have disappeared.

Uncle Jemmy Jenkin He seems to have done tutwork and general maintenance work on the 'owners account'. When Machine Shaft was choked with debris from above the 60fm level Jenkin went with Captain

Thomas and Abram to inspect the problem. On August 14 1823 Petherick wrote: *I've sett the job to hole to 50 & clear the level & put in footway to Uncle Jemmy Jenkin & pare for £4, they have rose 5 or 6 feet & have not yet hol'd.* That night Thomas reported: *I saw Jenkin's men to night they have hol'd the rise to the 50 level, it's a good job to have a road in safety.* A week later Thomas said Abram and Jenkin had put in a launder to divert the water on the 40fm level and had sufficient ladder to put in a manway under the 50fm level, but for some reason they were not happy. Three days later is was stated that Uncle Jemmy Jenkin and Young Jemmy were going to work with Tom Spargoe.

William Jenkin(s) He was a tributer whose pitch was over the 90fm level close to Mark Terril's, John Vincent's and Goldbey's pitches. They were working in the eastern part of the Valley Lode. On March 18 1823 Thomas visited these pitches and commented that Goldby's and Jenkin's pitches were poor. Three weeks later Petherick visited the pitch and it had improved considerably. There was a *good branch or ore in the back of the 90 which I was very glad to see.* On June 10 Thomas again visited Jenkin's pitch and again it was described as poor. On September 25 Petherick told Thomas of another potential boundary dispute between tributers. *I expect you'll see Mark Terrill & pare about a part of William Jenkin's pitch, which Jenkin & pare are not willing to give up. Jenkin wishes to keep his ground as far down as the 110.* The copper grade seems to have improved again and Jenkin clearly wanted to continue to work the ground below his pitch to the 110fm level.

John Jewell The sole reference to John Jewell was in the entry by Captain Petherick on July 4 1823: *I believe John Jewell & ptrs have rather burnt their fingers in taking in the South ore with 14lbs, but they are taught this lesson by experience & they will not easily forget it I shou'd think.* It is hard to say precisely what this means, but it sounds like they were tributers who had mixed their ore with some from the South Part of the Main Lode, although what is meant by 'with 14lbs' is hard to say!

Peter Knight The entry for March 13 says *Peter Knight complains against our cage*, and Petherick comments that Trumferey ought to repair it. It clearly refers to the 'cage' or drum of the whim engine, which was faulty or damaged.

(?) **Kit** No Christian name was given for Kit in either of the two mentions of him. He was a tutworker who appears to have been crosscutting through a wide lode in Entral workings. The entry by Petherick on July 2 1823 is worth quoting in full. *I've been down to Entrall today. Kit & pare are all in the old core again. They have driven only 3½ feet. They have left the good ground standing to the north & are got away to the south in very hard ground. Sollars all choak'd & end full of stuff, which according to custom Kit promis'd to clear against I came again. I told him he shou'd not work there any more if he did not be cleaner in his work & if he was hurted by means of the bad air he shou'd not be paid for it from the Club.* The 'sollars' referred to were floor sollars, which were laid as a false floor, beneath which the air could move back from the face. If the sollars were choked with dirt then the air would have no circuit and the end would not be ventilated. Petherick warned Kit, that should he be injured by the poor air he would not be given sick pay through the club, as he had been warned and it was his own bad practice which would have caused the problem. A month later Petherick was to visit Kit's end again, and he was nervous about it. *Tomorrow I'll go down to Entrall & measure Kit's end, who seems very uneasy on account of my being about to measure it over again.* Perhaps Kit had not cleaned the end up and the sollars were still choked.

(?) **Mankey** The only reference to Mankey (usually spelt Mankee in Camborne) was on June 4 1823. Mankey was a tributer who had had done well *and will have a good pay day on Saturday.* He and the Terrills had carried out some tutwork for which they were owed, but as Mankey had done well on his tribute contract the captains decided to hold over the tutwork payment till next time.

Uncle Michael (?) No surname was given. The prefix 'Uncle' used by the captains with some of the men suggests older, more experienced miners. Michael could have been a tributer, but he might equally have been a tutworker. The entry for February 11 1823 sounds like he was crosscutting on tutwork, and the entry for July 11 seems to confirm this possibility, as his ore was poor enough *to be put with the halvans,* or low grade ore.

(?) **Marks** No Christian name was given in the single entry for Marks. On 11 April 1823 he was working with Tom Rogers and they were in some sort of trouble, serious enough to be taken to the purser, Willam Reynolds. He appears to have been Roger's partner in a tribute pitch on the 110fm level. (See Tom Rogers below)

Nathaniel The only reference to Nathaniel was by Captain Petherick on the night of 26 May 1823. *Tell Nathaniel to get the carpenters to repair the pulley at Machine (Shaft) & let him oil & grease the pullies.* He appears to have been some sort of maintenance man or mechanical fitter.

Neddy Nicholas He was a tutworker. On 23rd September 1823 he was referred to as driving a crosscut to intersect Roskear Broaze Lode. His mate was James Rowe. It appears to have been important to the mine for the lode to be cut soon, as William Petherick comments: *No lode no pay.*

James (Jem) Oppy He worked mainly on tribute, but also did some tutwork and occasionally worked on the 'owners account'. On 12 March 1823 Oppy asked for a man called Jeffery to replace William Crase in his pare. Two days later Petherick reported that Jem Oppy had brought in a sample from South Valley Shaft and he was *as big as bull's beef* over it. That night Captain Thomas dismissed Oppy's claim, and said he had stolen the sample from James James' pitch. On 12 May Thomas reported that Jeffery, Oppy and partners were cheerful because they had holed a shaft they were driving toward. They had drilled five foot into it with a 'boyer' or drill steel. Thereafter, Petherick expressed concern for the future earnings of Oppy and his mates. *What shall us do respecting James Oppy & pare. It appears to me that next month they will be oblig'd to shit small turds.* Four days later, on June 2, Captain Petherick arranged for Oppy and his pare to take a sett on the 100fm level, *the bargain includes 5fms in the East End.* On 10 July Oppy had a problem with hoisting his dirt, for when he and his mates went down to fill the kibble they were held up by the shaft being left covered by Dick Thomas and his pare on the previous shift, causing a delay for Oppy whilst he cleared the shaft. On 26 August Captain Petherick visited Oppy's end on the 100fm level, which he surveyed and measured. The final reference to James Oppy was on 8 September when *Old Tom Crase* demanded to know why Petherick *didn't put his son with Oppy & pare & if I wouldn't put him there he wou'd go to Captn Rule & from there to Mr Reynolds & he wou'd see whether he cou'dn't get employ for his son or not ... he went off in a great rage I believe swearing.*

Thomas Oppy He was a tributer. The first reference is in the entry for 18 December 1822, when Captain Thomas reported that Oppy and pare spent the night breaking rocks so that they could fill the kibbles for hoisting to surface. They would start hoisting their ore the following night. Two days later Captain Petherick commented that Tom Oppy's pitch appeared to be failing. His tribute pitch was on the 134fm level, and on the 13 January 1823 Captain Petherick visited it, commenting on the *very bad ground about the shaft at the 134*.

James Pascoe He was one of those mine workers whose job or status is hard to define. Theoretically, he and his men were employed by the mine for specific tasks normally undertaken by men on the 'owners account'. However, from the more than two-dozen references to him and his men, between January and October 1823, it is apparent that the tasks they were assigned were almost always paid at an agreed amount for each job – hence, they were in effect tutworkers. For example, on 9 January Captain Thomas mentioned that the manager agreed that for clearing attle from a crosscut and throwing it onto the stulls, Pascoe and his men should be paid £20–£25. That night Petherick commented that the job should take at least 5 weeks and that £25 was fair – despite Pascoe's demand for £40. The mine captain added that they should also be paid 10s tribute for ore they separated whilst clearing the crosscut. In March Pascoe and partners cleared North Valley Shaft of debris so that hoisting could restart. They asked for £9 for the task but after some haggling they accepted £8. In April another such job was priced at £7. This illustrates the point that defining miners into set categories is impossible.

The variety of work carried out by Pascoe and his men is interesting. On 6 January 1823 they were building a timber staging to enable them to clear attle which was choking the workings. Two days later they were ready to run the attle from the blocked shaft to new stulls. Eight men were employed on the task. On 9 January they were engaged in clearing out a crosscut on the 118fm level and thowing the waste rock onto the stulls. Captain Petherick described the enormous rocks being cleared: *Saw Pascoe & ptrs throwing deads like sons of bitches at 118 – went to examine the state of the stulls up over them west of Valley Shaft at 110 on North Part.* On 21 February Captain Thomas wrote: *I was up with Pascoe & ptrs in the Roarer*

(Lode) – I suppose they will make a finish of the job next week, there is a large lode going west, mixt with ore & tin. They were, apparently, clearing the level so that the tributers could work there. In March Pascoe and his gang were working with Abram and Crase the timbermen, clearing debris from North Valley Shaft, so that ore could be hoisted. They were clearing deads from the 145fm level and there was some discussion as to whether it was easier to take the dirt to surface or to the stulls over the 118fm level. Throughout April Pascoe was engaged in clearing the 145 level and sending the dirt to surface. In June Pascoe had to supply men to help drive a north crosscut through extremely hard 'irestone' or elvan – six men were needed and they were only progressing two fathoms a month – six inches a day! In early August they were putting in a new ladderway ('footway') and by the end of the month they were driving 134fm level, on tutwork.

The September entries add to what we know about James Pascoe. He had a daughter who was a bal maiden at the mine, and she was one of a group who were fired because one of them had stolen a whim rope and no one would confess or inform. Shortly thereafter, Captain Petherick noticed her name on the pay sheets and angrily enquired why she was being employed when she had been dismissed? The girl had apparently gone to Wheal Bryant section of the mine and been taken on again, eliciting outraged sarcasm from the younger mine captain. James Pascoe was also among the several Docloath miners who were occasionally 'moon lighting' at Captain Thomas' Bolenowe Mine. The final entry for James Pascoe was for the night of 6 October 1823, and tells us that he and his men, together with Tom Davis and partners, were clearing the 80fm level and that Pascoe was the 'taker' – the one in charge.

Josey Perkin He was only mentioned once but there was no indication of his job. The reference only says that he was fat.

Richard Prideaux He was a tributer. Little is said about him in the journal. On 12 May 1823 Captain Petherick wrote that: *Richard Prideaux & pare want to have the tinstuff cleared away from their pile that they may begin to spal theirs.* It would appear that either Prideaux had tin ore in with his copper, and wanted it cleared so that he could break the copper ore up for hoisting, or that another tributer's tin ore was mixed with or close to his copper ore and he wanted it removed. The only other reference to Richard Prideaux was by Petherick on the 8 September, when he commented that the miner was 'now tolerably well satisfied respecting his tribute'. There is no hint as to where his pitch was.

William Pryor He was a tributer. On 5 August 1823 Captain Thomas said that Captain Rule had sett several tribute pitches including one to William Pryor at 10s in the pound. Captain Thomas names Pryor's mates as John Jeffrey, Abey Skewes and James Rule. Pryor probably lived at Bollenowe because after the accident to Matthew and John Harris, when Matthew was killed and John apparently injured, William Pryor was asked to take John's 'club money' to him. The Harrises lived at Bolenowe.

William Pryor Junior He probably worked on the owners' account and appears to have been the son of William Pryor described above. On 10 June 1823 Captain Thomas gave Pryor the task of constructing a ladder road. *I have put William Pryor Jnr to make a road to come to Valley Ladder Road and when he has done that he will Repair the road to the shaft to bring kibbles, etc etc.*

(?) Rablin He appears to have been a tributer. The only mention of him was 18 August 1823 when Captain Thomas told Petherick he was going to *put in Rablin's ore with Richard Thomas's.*

William Richards He was a tributer. Richards had the nickname 'Daniel' for some reason. Normally, if two men had the same name the mine accounts would use one of their nicknames to differentiate them. William Richards was suspected of trying to *pull a fast one* with his tribute contract. Captain Petherick wrote on 25 August 1823: *William Richards (Daniel) was saying to me about going with Frankey Rule & ptrs in John Vincent's place, but I think as they were so uncommonly eager to split the pitches they shou'd remain so, because Frankey & pare have a little ore more than is in their pitch, they want to go back again & in the course of a month we shall have the trouble of separating the pitches once more.* This sounds very much like tributers with adjacent pitches moving ore from one pitch to another to get a better price for it – and sharing the profits! The notorious 'patchiness' of Camborne lodes might also have been the reason for the tributers wanting to split a pitch, which was poor in one part and rich in another. By bidding high for what had been a poor pitch they might get a high tribute for the part which was rich. Whatever the fiddle was Captain Petherick sought to prevent it so that the mine was not the loser.

Nicky 'Hick' Richards Tributer's mate. The nickname 'Hick' is interesting because it has been a derivative of Richard(s) in Cornwall since Medieval times (Fox & Padel Arundells p.cxxxii). On 25 August 1823 Captain William Petherick wrote to Captain Thomas: *I've been down to Entral today – nothing new. There has been a little noise here today between the young Nicky Richards Hick & Tom Spargoe. Henry Adams tells me that there was an agreement made before you by Thomas Spargoe that he shou'd employ Nicky for this week. Uncle Jemmy Jenkin & the young Jemmy are going with Tom Spargoe. What's become of John Jenkin I don't know. I wish you wou'd say what the agreement is that I may settle it in the morning between them.* Once again the two mine captains were called in to arbitrate between disputing miners. (see Nicky Richards Hick above)

Tom Roberts He was a tributer who carried out other tasks, usually related to his workplace. On 9 January 1823 Roberts and others were clearing stuff out of a crosscut near to South Valley Shaft. In February Roberts and his mates had their account settled for timbering they had done in December. They had timbered over their ore pass and put in a stull at the 118fm level. In March Captain Thomas reported that Rogers' pitch on 110fm level North Lode had had *another grand run*, but the dirt had, unfortunately, lodged on Tom Roberts' stull at the 118 level.

On the night of 12 May Captain Petherick informed Captain Thomas of a difficult problem which needed sorting out. *While I think of it & have a little time on hand, it may not be amiss to give you my thoughts respecting T Roberts. You know they have two pitches amongst them, one copper the other tin. At certain times I know they have all been working the copper pitch while the tin pitch has been left idle & vice versa. Now I do not think this is as it shou'd be, as they shou'd in my opinion, confine themselves either to the one or the other, because its waiting for any advantage which may arise in either pitch – consequently the other will be immediately deserted. Shou'd it so happen, as above suppos'd, all the blame will fall upon us – they will of course always work the best pitch leaving us to scramble out of any dilemma into which we may get by allowing them so great a latitude, directly contrary to the Rules of the Mine & to the discouragement of all our Tributers who ought to have as much privilege & encouragement as T Roberts & pare for anything that I can see.* The following day Thomas replied: *I shall go down thro' Roberts's pitches tomorrow & will soon settle the business with them about having two pitches.* It was to be nearly three months before the problem of the two pitches was sorted out, the miners clearly having the best of the argument in the interim. On 8 August Captain James Thomas told Captain Petherick: *Thomas Roberts & ptrs desire me to speak to Captain Rule about their throwing their pitches together 13s 4d & 4s, as they intend to take down the side under where Tom Rogers work'd. I lay'd the case before both Captain Rules and they consented at once that the whole ground be worked at 8s 8d.*

The only other mention of Tom Roberts was on the night of 12 June, when Petherick commented that, *Tom Roberts & others have been working out of core this evening very smartly.* Was this overtime at the end of their core (shift) or were they working an extra shift?

Sampson ('Sampy' or 'Sammy') Roberts He was a tributer. Until August 1823 Sampy Roberts' pitch was in a stope close to Gossan Shaft at the 80fm level. In March there was a serious problem at Gossan Shaft, where a large piece of ground and a lot of attle was ready to fall into the shaft at the 40fm level. Roberts and other tributers whose pitches were threatened were ordered to carry out repairs to the timbering at the shaft. They were also told to put a ladder road in over the 40 level at North Valley Shaft, due to the problem at Gossan. In early June Roberts carried out some more timbering, presumably to protect his pitch from sinking attle above the 80fm level. On 10 June Captain Thomas wrote: *Sam's Roberts's pitch – sinking under the 80 – poor.* In August Petherick suggested that Thomas *see Sampy Roberts about a pitch at W W* (Water Whim Shaft).

Richard Rogers He was a tributer. The only reference to Rogers was in the entry for 3 March 1823, when Captain Thomas said he was going to grant a pitch to him *to the west of Hs.* What this alludes to is a mystery.

Thomas Rogers He was a tributer. On 23 December 1822 Captain Thomas visited Rogers' pitch on the 110fm level and described it and the adjacent stopes as *very dangerous places*. Three weeks later Captain Petherick also had a look at Rogers' pitch and pronounced it *as dangerous as any*. The danger was caused by attle thrown onto stulls above the 110fm level continually sinking. Problems continued for Tom Rogers and his pare, for on the night of 5 February 1823 Petherick remarked: *"I believe we shall find Tom Rogers & ptrs in the dog watch this time – when you see them please give them a caution about their dressing cost which is uncommonly heavy, I believe all is not well there.* It appears that Rogers and his men were not sorting their ore sufficiently, or sending up inferior material for dressing. In March there was another run of ground at Rogers' workplace, this time the dirt had lodged on Tom Roberts' stull above the 118fm level. In April and September 1823 Rogers was involved in disciplinary moves by the management. In April the pare were ordered to stop working while the purser, Mr Reynolds, decided on the mine's course of action. Whatever action was taken Rogers was still working his pitch on the 110 level in June. In September he and Peter Grangey (see above) were caught out in a major breach of Dolcoath's rules and were again taken before the purser: *Peter Grangey & Rogers & all the whole tote of them were all turn'd off today by Mr Reynolds for a sett of Rogues & Vagabonds.* By this time Rogers had taken a new pitch – *John Bennett's old pitch* – and Petherick thought they were well suited to the place. Presumably, Tom Rogers and some of his mates were still tempted to sail close to the wind, and once again found themselves in trouble with the mine management.

John Rogers He was a tributer. The only reference to him was on 29 May 1823 when William Warren proposed to take Rogers' pitch with his four man pare, and Captain Petherick said that he was in favour of it.

James Rowe He was a tutworker. Between early January and late September 1823 there are five references to Rowe, and the one, for 8 September 1823, shows Rowe driving a crosscut in Roskear Broaze section of the mine. Captain Petherick wrote: *I've been to R Broaze today & sett a bargain to James Rowe & Temby to take out plank & send them up – their Xcut is hard but it tears well owing to a good head on the east side. Lode in the east end is very kindly with good spots of ore & very good ground with two smooth walls & really if that lode does not make ore I don't know where to fix on a kindlier one.* A fortnight later Petherick again refers to the lode: *I've put Neddy*

Nicholas to cut the R Broaze S(outh) Lode – no lode no pay – & James Rowe with him – Temby it seems is sick & never gave his comrade any notice of it & so obliged him to lose his days work yesterday & today the same. Little sympathy expressed for the sick Temby, but Rowe had a new mate to replace him, and despite two working days lost, the mine captain remained optimistic about the value of the lode.

Franky Rule He was a tributer. The only reference in the journal to Rule, was when he and his partners wished to go with William Richards to work John Vincent's former pitch. Captain Petherick was not enthusiastic about the proposal, although he gave no reason.

James Rule He was a tributer. On 5 August 1823 Captain Thomas reported that the manager, Captain John Rule, had sett two pitches *up in the ball today – 10s each – John Vial & his pare is gone in one of them & William Pryor & John Jeffrey – Abey Skewes & James Rule in the other.* There were also four unnamed miners on the contract, so that eight men worked each pitch.

John Rule Junior He was a tributer. On 14 August Petherick went underground in Entral section to estimate the tonnage and value of the ore waiting to be moved to the shaft and hoisted to surface. The mine captain estimated John Rule's ore as weighing roughly 4 tons and worth £6 11 6s a ton, which totalled over £26 6s.

Richard Rule No indication of his job, as the only mention of him was when Abraham the timberman spoke to him about what was tied up to *Tom Trythall's belly*, in September 1823.

William Rule He was a Tributer. The only mention of him was on 5 August 1823 when Captain Thomas remarked that William Rule and partners were to keep Abey Skewes' tribute pitch.

Abey Skewes He was a tributer. On 5 August 1823, in company with John Jeffery, James Rule and William Pryor, Skewes took a tribute pitch at 10s in the pound. His old pitch was taken by his former partner William Rule (see above).

(?) Smith No Christian name was given for Smith and no indication of his job. The sole reference to him was on 16 January 1823 when he returned with Henry Vincent from giving evidence, apparently, against 'the maid Eudey', presumably at the assizes at Bodmin. The two men were cold and stiff after their journey and asked for money to buy a drink and warm up. This suggests that they were giving evidence on behalf of the mine against Eudey.

(?) Stephen No Christian name was given for him. He appears to have been an underground labourer who carried out a variety of tasks, and probably worked as a day labourer on the 'owners' account'. On 14 January 1823 he and a miner called George were employed filling kibbles underground at Roskear Broaze Shaft. There were problems with hoisting sufficient dirt up the shaft and Captain Petherick sarcastically said that *if they carry on the way they are it will take them till midsummer to clear the ore.* They also needed a larger kibble. In April Petherick sent *Stephen down in the adit to sound it & find we are good deal nearer than when I last sounded it.* Presumably, the adit was close to 'holing through' either to a shaft or to a tunnel being driven toward it. Sounding was a primitive but effective way of discovering how close a holing was by listening to the drills being struck on the far side of the wall rock.

Thomas Spargoe/Spargo He was a tributer. He had a tribute pitch above the 80fm level on East Valley Lode. Prior to Spargoe taking it in April 1823, the pitch had been worked by a tributer called Goldsworthy, who was not pleased that Spargoe had taken it over. It seems that Spargoe had undercut Goldsworthy's bid at the setting. Spargoe worked well there and on 6 May Petherick reported: *I've been down today through South Valley, the shaft is not hol'd. Saw Spargoe & ptrs in Goldsworthy's pitch, they seem to work with some spirit.* In June Captain James Thomas described Spargoe's pitch above the 80fm level as *not rich but kindly ground.* Three weeks later Spargoe was asking for payment for timbering done by him and his pare *for driving laths and clearing the 100fm level.* Thomas agreed. Laths or planks were driven behind shaft timbers or stulls to keep back attle or weak and broken ground. In August there was a dispute with Henry Adams over Spargoe's alleged promise to take on Nicky Richards for a week. (see above)

(?) Sparnon He was a tributer. The sole mention of Sparnon was by Captain Thomas when he wrote on 3 March 1823 that he had sett

Sparnon's old tribute pitch to William Vincent and partners.

Dick Temby He worked as a tutworker and a tributer. On 2 January 1823 Temby was working as a tributer below the 118fm level. Captain Petherick wrote: *Abraham says he can get a plenty of attle to fill up Dick Temby's place from a Xcut at 118, which is gone North to the Roarer Lode & is all full of attle. Temby & ptrs shut a hole today in a rock which had fallen down & the report of the hole brought down some more of the ground, so the sooner we fill it up the better.* In June there was a problem with the timbering of North Valley Shaft, and Captain Petherick ordered Abraham and Crase to repair it, as its condition was threatening hoisting there. He then appears to blame Dick Temby for the problem: *I think Dick Temby & pare did it on purpose & if another run shou'd take place it's likely we shall loose the shaft altogether.* Presumably, the attle contained enough copper ore to make it worthwhile for Temby to cause it to run into his pitch – and he was unconcerned about the risk to the nearby shaft! On 29 July Petherick said: *I've marked the adit end. Temby & pare are too fond of short cores I think to do much there, however they have a bargain & as they have now no water to draw, they must work to get any money – there's a very fine lode in the end & flookan goes bigger as it goes east.* Temby and pare had been moved from the deeper levels up to the adit level at Roskear Broaze to drive a crosscut toward a lode. They were still there over two months later. On 8 September Captain Petherick reported: *I've been down R(oskear) Broaze today & sett a bargain to James Rowe & Temby to take out plank & send them up. Their X cut is hard but it tears well owing to a good head on the east side – lode on the east side is very kindly with good spots of ore & very good ground with two smooth walls.* Petherick was sanguine about the prospects on the lode, believing it showed every sign of being of value. A fortnight later Temby went off sick, and again the mine captain is critical: *Temby it seems is sick & never gave his comrade any notice of it & so oblig's him to lose his days work yesterday & today.* Captain Thomas replied that night: *I hear that Temby is very bad.* Five days later, on the night of 30 September Petherick was again criticising Temby: *The kibble has been sent down to Dick Temby & ptrs a score times tonight & not fill'd at all. I understand that before they went down they said they shou'd not be particular in looking out for it & I rather expect that this is willfull neglect.*

Between June and September 1823 Captain William Petherick accused

Dick Temby of deliberately risking the safety of an important hoisting shaft; being lazy and working *short cores*; of malingering when he went sick and being guilty of *willfull neglect* when sending up half empty kibbles. The young mine captain clearly did not like or trust Dick Temby.

James Terrill He was either a tutworker or tributer. The first mention of him was on 7 April 1823, when Captain Petherick wrote: *10/s to James Terrill's account – I think they deserve it all.* On 2nd June Petherick said: *James Terrill & ptrs have been down here today – one of their boys is gone & they can't get another for the same wages, so I told them I thought it best they shou'd take a man with them, which they have done.* It appears that Terrill was not making much on his contract and although Petherick was sympathetic, he was not particularly helpful.

John Terrill He was a tributer. He worked with Mark Terrill (below) and was almost certainly related to him. The only mention of John was on 4 June 1823 when Captain Petherick reported that he had forgotten to enter some tutwork owed to John and Mark Terrill. John and Mark were paid £9 in lieu of the tutwork owed.

Mark Terrill He was a tributer. In December 1822 he was working a pitch on one of the south lodes close to Water Whim Shaft (Eastern/Valley), below the 100fm level. Captain Thomas described the lode, which was also worked by John Vincent in an adjacent pitch, as *a branch of good gray ores about 4 or 5 inches big (wide).* He said that both pares were *sinking after under the 100fm level, East & West of W(ater) Whim Shaft.* Thomas spoke to the manager to ask if they could drive a crosscut on the 110fm level to prove the lode there. Captain Rule said they would discuss it further. A fortnight later, on 23 December, Captain Thomas again visited these stopes, inspecting William Jenkin's, John Vincent's and Mark Terrill's pitches, before climbing down to the 110fm level crosscut. Presumably this was the crosscut Thomas asked permission to extend to the lode being worked on 100 level. On March 18 1823 Captain James Thomas went to the stope being worked by Vincent and Terrill to settle a dispute over the boundary between their pitches. *I have measured their ground & made a mark for their boundary.* In June Captain Petherick remarked that he had forgotten to enter in the accounts some tutwork carried out by Mark and John Terrill.

John Terrill (see above) worked with Mark and was probably a relative. On 10 June Captain Thomas again visited the pitches of Jenkin, Vincent and Terrill: *Jenkin's pitch poor – down with Mark Terrill, small branch going west – John Vincent & ptrs is sinking opposite the + cut branch – about 4 inches ore and driving east branch small but good.* In August Captain Petherick told Captain Thomas that Mark Terrill wanted to keep their ore on *their own floor,* and he added that they expected to raise about 30 tons of ore. As there was frequent discussion about where a tributer's ore was dressed and sampled, it seems that the miners liked to keep their eye on their own dirt to ensure it was not mixed with inferior stuff. On 25 September there was another different kind of dispute between the tributers working below the 100 level at Water Whim Shaft. Petherick asked Thomas: *I expect you'll see Mark Terrill & pare about a part of William Jenkin's pitch, which Jenkin & pare are not willing to give up. Jenkin wishes to keep his ground as far down as the 110.* The ore shoot was obviously rich and Jenkin wanted it all for himself. However, the mine would benefit by having it broken by two pares of tributers, and hence removed that much faster.

Uncle Stephen Terrill He was a surface worker who was probably in charge of some of the stamps. The only mention of him was on 20 May 1823 when Captain Petherick wrote: *Uncle Stephen Terrill has brought in his book with the account of the stampt ore.* As the term 'Uncle' was used it is probable that he was an older man, this being the normal prefix for them.

Abraham Thomas Junior He appears to have worked on tribute with Thomas Spargoe on the 100fm level, for he is mentioned with Spargoe on that level, carrying out timbering work.

Benjamin Thomas He was a tributer. On 10 June 1823 Captain Thomas reported that he had been through the 110fm level crosscut and examined Benjamin Thomas' pitch and it was in a safe condition.

Davy Thomas He was a miner who worked as both tributer and tutworker. The first mention of Davy Thomas, in May 1823, was connected to Bolenowe Mine, when Captain Thomas said: *I am going home to see what is the best news of Bolenowe Mine. Davy Thomas dreamt of a fine course of ore & tin there.* Captain Petherick reacted with predictable sarcasm at James

Thomas' news, deriding such *dream lode* fantasies as pure rubbish. In August Davy was working a pitch below the 60fm level. An enormous quantity of attle *fell away from over the 60 in Machine Shaft and fill'd it about 8 or 10fms over 134 – it's a good job that Trezona nor D Thomas was not down*. With the pitches of Trezona and Thomas threatened, Captain Thomas reported the following day: *I have by Captain Rule's consent sett a bargain to John Trezona & ptrs & Davy Thomas & ptrs to put in timber over the stopes above the 134 near the Valley & to put back all the attle that is the Machine Shaft, which is about 10fms in height – £6 6s.* Clearly, Machine Shaft was quite close to Valley or North Valley Shaft, on the western side of the Red River valley, above Tuckingmill. On 24 September Captain Petherick requested Captain Thomas to return his dial which had been taken to Bolenowe Mine some time earlier. He suggested that either James Pascoe or Davy Thomas fetch it. This indicates either that Davy Thomas was still one of Captain Thomas' Bolenowe Mine 'moon lighters', or that Davy lived at Bolenowe and could pick the dial up on his way to work. The following day Captain Petherick refers to Davy and indicates that he was tributing for tin: *There ought to be a new rope put in tomorrow, that Davey Thomas & pare may draw their tinstuff tomorrow night otherwise they will not be able to sample it in time for pay day.* The tin ore appears to have come from a stope near North Valley and Machine shafts, between the 60 and 134fm levels.

Edward Thomas He was a tributer. The only entry which refers to Thomas shows that he was tributing near Gossan Shaft. On 28 August 1823 Captain Petherick wrote: *I've made out the calculations of ore with the exception of Edward Thomas's (Gossan) I suppose they will have 20 or more tons.* With so many Thomas' working underground Petherick differentiated by adding 'Gossan' to his name, so that his colleague would know to whom he referred.

John Thomas He was a tributer. His pitch was near to South Valley Shaft. On 20 December 1822 a dispute was reported involving John and Richard Thomas and James James over the limits of their respective pitches. Three days later Captain Thomas went underground to try to sort out the dispute, and he included Vine and partners in the argument. He *heard a great deal of confused talk. One said its so, the other 'Thee art a liard', etc – but in the end of it I told them we should put the pitches together.* In May 1823 Petherick wrote: *We ought to put 2 men more with Dick Thomas – I think that John & Richard*

Thomas had better go there. It appears that 'Dick' Thomas was a tributer and John and Richard were younger miners. There were also two John Thomas' in Valley Section of the mine, and even the mine captains got confused about them. On 21 July Petherick said: *I see in our drawing book two John Thomas's & I've been thinking whether or not some of it does not belong to William Thomas or John Thomas S V (South Valley) or John Thomas W Whim (Water Whim)*.

John Thomas He was a tributer. The only mention of him appears to have been on 2t July 1823 by Captain Petherick, when he says he was confused as to which John Thomas he was entering in the books. He refers to a John Thomas working near Water Whim Shaft, as opposed to the one above at South Valley Shaft.

Richard (Dick)Thomas There was more than one Richard or Dick Thomas' in Valley section of Dolcoath. It would be difficult to decide which one is which. It appears that more than one of them was a tributer, and at least one of them worked from Gossan Shaft. As noted above (under John Thomas) the younger one worked with John Thomas and the one usually called Dick appears to have been an older man, perhaps the father of the other one.

Dick Thomas He was a surface copper dresser, probably a charge hand, shiftboss or 'grass captain', although the fact that he worked with a 'pare' suggests that he worked as a contract ore dresser, paid by how much ore was sorted and sampled. The only two references to Thomas are in connection with *Pascoe's daughter*. On 17 September 1823 Captain Petherick wrote that he was annoyed that she was working at the mine again: *I went out to take down the maiden's days this afternoon & was very much surprised to find Pascoe's daughter working with Dick Thomas & pare*. Captain Thomas replied that night, and mentioned that she had been working at Wheal Bryant, which was where Dick Thomas was in charge of ore dressing. Wheal Bryant lay toward the western end of the mine, between Dunkins Garden and Old Dolcoath.

Stephen Thomas He was described as 'the Halvan man' and was an ore dresser who seems to have specialised in dressing poor ore or 'halvans'. Half a century earlier William Pryce called halvans "the refuse Ore, or the poor

Ore ... after the prime Copper Ore or Crop is first taken out; but they often cull over these Halvans again, and take more Ore out ... called Halvan Ore." On the night of 19 February 1823 Captain Petherick wrote: *Trezona & ptrs fill'd their ore yesterday which they say is about a ton. As soon as it was drawn Stephen Thomas the Halvan man took possession of it but I believe he has not dress'd any of it. I don't know what we shall do with it unless we sell it to some one or other of the Halvan men or send it down to fire stamps, suppose you ask Capt'n Rule's advice on the subject.* Stephen Thomas appears to have worked for the mine, but the ore he dealt with, if it was considered too poor to waste time on, could be sold to outside independent 'halvan men'. If the stamps were used to reduce it the fines could produce economic amounts of copper worth smelting, but the subsequent washing might make it uneconomic.

William Thomas He was a tributer. On 3 March 1823 Captain Thomas visited the 40fm level at Gossan Shaft and noted a dangerous piece of ground and a large quantity of attle ready to fall into the shaft. He ordered Sampy Roberts and William Thomas to repair it. The mine captain also mentions that he had had ladders put into their *old place in the Valley Shaft over 40.* The next reference to William Thomas was on 28 April when Petherick reported: *I've set a pitch to William Thomas & ptrs (Tuckingmill) at Gossan on the South Valley Lode.* Once again, more than one person with the same name necessitated the use of a nickname. In this case it might have referred to where William Thomas lived – Tuckingmill. In June Thomas and his pare were paid for stems they worked outside their tribute contract, in April, and in July Petherick mentions a mistake in the predicted ore tonnage. *I think we shall have near 110 tons Bal Ore – the increase is owing to William Thomas & ptrs (Tuckingmill) having giv'n us a wrong Calculation of their ore – I suppose they will have 24 tons produce 10.* The last entry for William Thomas is dated 21st July (night) 1823 and again uses his nickname 'Tuckingmill'. *I have left out William Thomas's Tuckingmill's drawing for two reasons, the first is because the landers at Gossan have turn'd in some of his drawing at South Account House ... the second is because in our Drawing Book are two John Thomas's & I've been thinking whether or not some of it does not belong to William Thomas.* Once again there was confusion over too many miners with the same name.

William Tippet He was a tributer. The sole mention of him was on 5 August 1823, when he and several others were sett pitches by Captain Rule at 10s in the pound. The entry mentions that there were to be 8 men in each pare.

Dick Trezona He was a tutworker. It appears likely that he worked with John Trezona, who was probably a relative. (see below) On the night of 26 May 1823 Captain Petherick asked Capt Thomas: *Does Dick Trezona work at Bolenoe – he has not been here this long time & they have not been working but one core in the end.* The next day Thomas replied: *Trezona's end is hard & ugly – I ask'd them about Dick – he has been up a few stems with Mr Daniel – at South Bolenowe.* That night an angry Captain Petherick asked: *Did you know of Dick Trezona's being at South Bolenoe – they kept it a most wonderful secret from me, indeed if I had not discover'd it for myself & that too quite by accident, perhaps I shou'd never have known it. If Dick has not your consent to go he never had mine & I think if that is the case he must have our consent to stay away. I do not like such little mean tricks at all & that Dick is a first rate shaver is as notorious as the sun at noon day – but enough of Dick & all such scamps.* Like other miners, Trezona was not above a little 'moon lighting' in another mine, especially as the end he was driving at Dolcoath was *hard & ugly*.

John (Jan) Trezona He was a tutworker. He spent most of the period crosscutting toward a lode close to North Valley Shaft. The first mention of John Trezona was on 9 January 1823, when Captain Thomas climbed down to the 200fm level in the 'Middle District' (Bullen Garden) with Captain Tregoning to look at *some good tin* there. He climbed back up to the 145 level and walked back to the Valley Section through *a level of mud & stuf*, where he examined Trezona's end and noted that it was much as the last time he had seen it. On the 13 Petherick visited Trezona's drive and reported: *I've been down today – Trezona's end is not looking so well for ore or tin, but the ground is far better if it holds untill Survey Day as it is now. We must lower the their price considerably – the hard stone appears to be nearly all gone.* Typical of the young mine captain, as soon as the rock seems easier to work he wants to reduce the price per fathom paid to the miner. The ore in the end did not improve, and on the night of 19 February Petherick told Thomas that Trezona had sent up a ton of poor copper ore which was sent straight to Stephen Thomas, the 'Halvan Man'. Two days later Captain Thomas said that Trezona's end contained *ore & mundick* and could not be far from the lode. On the night of 21 February Petherick spoke of a problem which he and *Old Captain Tucker* had, and comments, rather mysteriously, *Henry Vincent nor Jan Trezona are not men I think that will put up with things of that kind*. He then adds: *The last time I was down with Trezona & ptrs I thought they had cut an eastern part – of course not the right one*. Three days later the mine captain wrote: *Please to observe the sketch of Trezona's end. I think we had better drive east a little on that part which they have in their end – don't let Captain Rule know anything about it*. Cautiously, the older captain failed to instruct Trezona to do as Petherick suggested, probably not wanting to risk the manager's wrath: *I have not told Trezona & ptrs to drive east as I did not recolect it*. On 3 March Captain Thomas again visited Trezona: *I have been down thro' Valley today, measured Trezona's end – there is some good bits of ore in it with a large quantity of mundick*. A week later Petherick again inspected the end: *I've been down to N(orth) Valley to day – Trezona's end appears to be near the lode by the great variety of substances which compose*. On the 13th Petherick again visited the end and reported that it was *much the same*, as he did a fortnight later, and again ten days after that. On 27 May Captain Thomas visited Jan Trezona's workplace, and asked about the whereabouts of Dick Trezona (see above) and was told he was working at South Bolenowe Mine – 'moon lighting'. The end was described as *hard & ugly*. In June Petherick needed extra men to drive the 42fm level north crosscut through 'irestone' and elvan, which was very hard. They needed six men on the drive and the captain suggested that they take two of them from either James Pascoe or Jan Trezona. In August there was a major rock fall in Machine Shaft, close to North Valley Shaft, and the mine captain remarked that it was fortunate that John Trezona and others who worked below were not at work when it happened. As it was their workplace which was threatened by the fall, Trezona and Davy Thomas, together with their pares, were given a bargain to timber over the stopes above the 134fm level, and remove the attle which had choked Machine Shaft.

Tom Trythall The two entries are vague about his job, which might not have been underground and might even have been in the office, but there was a humorous reference to him. *Abram … told Richard Rule & me today that of all the things that ever he saw in his life he never saw such a thing before as there is ting'd up to Tom Trythall's belly*. Tinged is a Cornish dialect word for being 'tied up', so we can only imagine to what part of Tom Trythall Abram was referring.

John Vial He was a tributer. On 27 May 1823 Captain Thomas wrote: *John Vial & ptrs has been taking out timber today in the old bottoms west of Valley (Shaft), there is several good pieces there.* In July Captain Petherick commented that he had made a mistake when he entered Vial's stems and tutwork on his tribute account, and added that Vial should be paid £9 which was owed him. In August Captain Thomas reported that the manager had sett a tribute pitch to John Vial at 10s in the pound.

William Vial He was a tutworker. On 24 February 1823 Captain Petherick told the older mine captain: *Captain Rule says to be sure to see William Vial & ptrs & put them to sink in the place which I pointed out to Willey the last time I was down there & for them to begin to sink directly.* Thomas replied the following day: *I have been down thro' Entral today – Vial & ptrs has begun to sink under 70 about 6fm behind the end – the lode seems to be about a foot big – the 70 west is wet and hard.* On 7 April Petherick said that he had entered 10s in the book for ore raised to grass from William Vial's workplace. Presumably this ore was from the winze which Vial was sinking under the 70fm level, in Entral.

Henry Vincent Junior There is no indication of what his job was. On 6 January 1823 Captain Thomas reported: *I saw Henry Vincent Junior – his father's coffin cost 45/-, and say for all other expenses on the occasion 15/- or 20/- more – I don't think it wou'd be out of the way – mind to put it in the book.* Ten days later Petherick reported that Henry Vincent and one Smith had returned from court, having apparently given evidence against the *maid Eudey*, who was convicted of some crime. The two men were cold and stiff and asked for money for a pint – *Henry is stuttering already & Smith is as stiff as a poker.* In February Petherick mentioned that Henry Vincent was involved in some dispute in which *Old Capt Tucker* of Wheal Francis was concerned. There is no indication as to what the problem was.

John Vincent He was a tributer who also carried out tutwork. The first mention of John Vincent was dated 11 November 1822, but in fact it should have said 11 December. Captain Thomas visited Vincent's tribute pitch under the 100fm level on South Lode, near Water Whim Shaft. Another tributer, Mark Terrill was also sinking below the 100 level, with one working on the east and the other on the west side of the shaft. Thomas reckoned the lode looked good. On 23 December the mine captain again visited the stopes where Vincent was working and everything was as before. He climbed down through to the 110fm level, which suggests that the lode had been opened up by a winze or a rise, which connected the two levels. In March Captain Thomas went through *the South Lode, settled a kind of dispute between John Vincent & ptrs & Mark Terrill about the limits.* Thomas measured the ground and marked the boundary between their two pitches. On 8 April there was another problem with Vincent's workplace. When Captain Petherick visited his pitch Vincent insisted *that it's not the right lode.* The suspicious mine captain commented: *They will get as much money this last two months as the two months before & we shall be murderd or serv'd some ugly trick or other.* How John Vincent was to gain an advantage by his insistence that he was sinking on the wrong lode or branch, we do not know. Clearly, the young mine captain thought the branch being worked would give the tributers as good a return as they had previously enjoyed. Captain Thomas answered Petherick's concern with the comment: *If I shou'd think we was to be murderd or serv'd some worse trick, because Vincent & ptrs is likely to get some money on this one, we are better to tell them to give some off it to some poor Tributer that has not got his subsist.* Whatever the complaint against Vincent was, both mine captains were convinced the miner would continue to do well in the pitch he working. On 19 June Thomas reported that Vincent was still working his original pitch below the 100fm level: *sinking opposite the + cut branch – about 4 inches ore and driving east branch – small but good.* It is not clear whether the drive was on tribute or tutwork. In July Captain Petherick told Thomas that Peter Abram, another tributer, wanted his ore sampled with that of John Vincent and other tributers. He did not say why. The final reference to John Vincent was on 25 August, when Petherick reported that William 'Daniel' Richards wanted to go with Frankey Rule and his pare into John Vincent's place, but as the mine captain had already had problems with these two tributers, he was reluctant to let them take the pitch.

William Vincent He was a tributer. The only mention of William Vincent was in the entry for 3 March 1823, where Captain Thomas wrote: *I have sett Sparnon's old pitch to William Vincent & ptrs.* There is no mention as to where this pitch was.

Stephen Vine He was a tributer. On 23 December 1822 Captain James

Thomas went underground through Water Whim Shaft to sort out a dispute between Stephen Vine and James James, in which insults were exchanged. The mine captain said he would put their two pitches together, as they could not sort themselves out. That night Captain Petherick commented that now their pitches were consolidated they appeared to be content. He described the tributers as like *young consols* in their disputations, even continuing to argue after they both admitted that it was all *worth nothing*. On the night of 3 June 1823 Captain Thomas told Captain Petherick that Stephen Vine had taken a pitch in Entral, which was *not of much consequence*. Thomas explained to Petherick that Vine was willing to give up his pitch and go to work at Bolenowe Mine, as he needed a man there. Vine asked to Thomas to check with the other mine captain to ensure that it was all right for him to go. The next day Petherick replied: *Stephen Vine took his pitch on condition of leaving it when he pleas'd – if that had never been the case he shou'd (not) have liberty to go when he pleas'd.* Petherick did not appear happy that a Dolcoath tributer could so easily leave his contract and go to work in a nearby mine – even if he did have a share in it!

William Warren He was a tributer. On 29 May 1823 Captain Petherick went down Entral. He said that William Warren and his four man pare had proposed that they take John Roger's former pitch there, on the 52fm level, and the mine captain said that he had *no great objection to them having it*. A few days later Petherick discussed with Warren the limits of the pitch, and Warren asked that it be *limited 15fms west of the + course, that they might work old Crowder's bottoms*. He asked Thomas if there was any objection to this. Thomas replied: *I think that Warren & ptrs might go 15fms west of + course, so they may clear the old bottoms, that we may see what is going down.* Once cleared, the mine captain could examine the lode at the bottom of the stope and get an idea of its value. On 23 July Captain Thomas went down Entral Shaft and visited Warren's pitch at the 52fm level, which were *covered with water – ends of ground poor*. The last mention of William Warren in the journal was on 14 August, when Captain Petherick reported: *I've been down Entral today, I think Henry Davey will have 20 tons, William Warren 14 tons & John Rule Junior 4 tons, worth altogether about £250.* This makes Warren's 14 tons worth over £92. If the tribute was the average 10s in the pound, then the five man tribute pare averaged over £9 each from it. Of course, there is no indication of how long it took to break that 14 tons of ore.

THE BAL MAIDENS

Peggy Bennetts She appears to have been a surface supervisor of some sort. Probably a charge-hand over a group of bal maidens. On 15 October 1823 she asked Captain Rule, the manager, for *a man by night & a woman by day* to assist her, these to be clear of all usual charges and expenses. The following night Captain Petherick requested that Captain Thomas send to Peggy Bennetts *for a basket* which had been used to carry *bread & cheese*. Whether this suggests that her job was more connected to the Account House than the dressing floors, is not certain.

Maid Eudey There is no indication of her job or where she worked. The only reference is to her being convicted of a crime at the assizes, and two Dolcoath miners went to give evidence. It is probable that she was a locally employed bal maiden.

Margaret Freeman She was a young bal maiden who worked on the copper dressing floors in the Valley section of Dolcoath. She lived near Troon and was a friend of Betsy Webster. On the night of July 1 1823 Captain Thomas saw her and her friend Betsy walking home from the fair with some young men at about midnight. They were near Troon.

Grace Harvey She was a bal maiden who complained that her charge-hand had short-changed her over her money. On 24 July 1823 Captain Petherick wrote: *I understand that Grace Harvey was here today discoursing very sharply with Enoch concerning some money which she says Enoch owes her, but which Enoch stoutly denies & says 'tis Johnson & not him.* No shrinking violet here!

Grace Mayne She was a bal maiden who worked at North Roskear Mine. She was caught by Captain Petherick as she was keeping watch for a group of North Roskear bal maids who were stealing anvils and hand barrows from Dolcoath dressing floors. When challenged by Captain Petherick she replied that she was *waiting for some one or other to come up from*

underground. The mine captain then *charged her with stealing barrows &*
anvils, which she denied. Grace Mayne was not easily overawed by authority,
despite the possibility of serious punishment if taken before the courts. She
was glib and defiant, which does not appear to have been unusual
characteristics of the local bal maidens.

Nancy (?) Only her Christian name was given. She was a *Count House*
woman. She worked as a cleaner, who also prepared food for the mine
captains and washed their underground clothes. The only reference to her
was by Petherick who said: *I gave Nancy the ham today & she clean'd the*
house. She probably was assistant to Betsy West.

(?) Pascoe She was only referred to as *Pascoe's daughter.* She was one of the
Valley bal maidens who were accused of stealing a whim rope. As none
confessed or informed on the thief, they were all fired. Pascoe went to the
other side of the mine and got another job on the dressing floors, much to
the fury of the young Captain Petherick. The older mine captain, however,
was not particularly upset by Miss Pascoe's re-employment.

Sheaby Whether this was her Christian or surname or just a nickname, we
do not know. She appears to have been a bal maiden. She was the girl
friend of Abraham, the senior timberman, and appears to have been quite
a fierce lady. When Abraham bragged that he was to take *three weeks round*
among the women, when he had finished the job he was on, Sheaby said she
would put hot lead in his ear, if he did. The context suggests that she
worked on the Valley copper dressing floors.

Jenny Stone She was a charge hand on the dressing floors and would have
had a gang of bal maidens working under her. She was accused of trying to
fiddle the hours of the maidens, but the mine captain was suspicious and
would not pay. Petherick wrote: *An attempt has been made to impose upon us*
by Jenny Stone. I knew what she was at altho' I took down the days as she call'd
them over – I've spaled her 5/s. The fine or 'spale' was transferred to the
surface mine captain's book. Captain Petherick commented on the
difficulty of getting accurate figures from Stone and others, and said that he
would *discharge them as fast as I find them.*

Patience Wills She seems to have been the girl friend of Captain Petherick. Captain Thomas ribbed the younger mine captain unmercifully about her. She was probably a bal maiden at Dolcoath Mine.

Betsy Webster She was a young bal maiden who worked in the Valley section of Dolcoath Mine. She lived near Troon and was a friend of Margaret Freemen. She was seen at Troon, walking home from the fair at midnight by Captain Thomas on July 1 1823, with Margaret and some young men.

Betsy West She was the lady in charge of the account house used by the two mine captains. She cooked their food, washed their clothes, ran errands for them, went to Camborne to buy food and liquor and generally looked after everything at the account house and changing rooms. She also was the mine captain's principal source of news, gossip and information about the doings of the bal maidens, details of funerals and what people said and wore, and anything else they wanted to know.

A SIMPLE GLOSSARY OF DIALECT AND MINING TERMS USED IN THE JOURNAL

Adit: Mine drainage tunnel

Anvil: Flat, metal plate on which the copper was crushed by bal maids with bucking hammers

Attle: Mine waste rock

Bowling Green: See Keal alley

Cayenne Pepper: Hot, red pepper

Couch: A suspended platform used for inspecting and repairing shafts

Cowal: A coal basket carried on the shoulder

Croust: The food eaten at the mid-shift break. In St Just called 'moszel'

Dial: Surveying instrument – an early theodolite with a compass and sometimes a level

Dowsen: Obscure – possibly, refers to 'dowsing', or divining with a rod for mineral lodes or water

Fathom: Six feet

Figgy pudding: A fruit pudding like a Christmas pudding

Flep: Hot drink of ale, brandy & sugar

Fork: When a mine is in fork the water has been drained to the sump

Furt: The anus of a cow or bull

Grocked: Punished

Holing engine: Some sort of device for holing through the final piece of ground between a shaft and a tunnel

Keal Alley: Kails/keels = skittles – usually in pub yard

Kindly ground: Not rich, but hopeful ore ground

Rearing: Timber planking to contain loose ground around shafts or ladderways

Shaver: One who sailed 'close to the wind'

Shiner: Sweetheart

Skipper: Maggot

Sollar: Cornish word for a floor. Referred to either a platform in a ladderway or to a false floor used to enhance ventilation in dead ends

Spale: A fine

Stave: A ladder rung

Stull: Timbers placed across stopes to carry waste rock – also large single 'stull pieces' of timber to support the hanging wall

Swigging: Ribbing, taking the rise out of someone

Van: The value of black tin is determioned by the use of a vanning shovel, whereby a skilled tin dresser places a measured quantity of crushed ore on the shovel and then washes the waste away by deft movement of the shovel. The black tin concentrate left is then measured

Whim: Usually pronounced 'whem' in Camborne-Redruth mining district. A winding engine, which was powered by horses, water or steam

BIBLIOGRAPHY

Books

Buckley, Allen, *The Story of Mining in Cornwall*, 2005, Cornwall Editions, Fowey

Buckley, J. A., *A Miner's Tale: The Story of Howard Mankee*, 1988, Penhellick Publications, Camborne

Burt, R., *John Taylor*, 1977, Moorland, Buxton

Harris, John, *My Autobiography*, 1883, Hamilton Adams & Co, London

Harris, T. R., *Dolcoath: Queen of Cornish Mines*, 1974, Trevithick Society, Camborne

Jenkin, A. K. H. *The Cornish Miner*, 1948, Allen & Unwin, London

Lean, T., *On the Steam Engine*, 1977, Bradford Barton, Truro

Morrison, T. A., *Cornwall's Central Mines: The Northern District*, 1980, Alison Hodge, Penzance

Morrison, T. A., *Cornwall's Central Mines: The Southern District*, 1983, Alison Hodge, Penzance

Noall, Cyril, *Cornish Mine Disasters*, 1989, Dyllansow Truran, Redruth

Oliver, Thomas, *Autobiography of a Cornish Miner*, 1914, Camborne Printing & Stationary Co., Camborne

Pigot & Company, *A New Commercial Directory: Devon & Cornwall (1823–24 & 1830)*

Thomas, A. C., *Christian Antiquities of the Parish of Camborne*, 1967, Camborne

Vincent, E. S., *Province of Cornwall 1751–1959* (Freemasonry), 1960, Netherton Worth, Truro

Articles

Dr J. A. Paris, 'On accidents which occur in the mines of Cornwall' (1817)

Dr S. P. Schwartz, 'The Making of a myth: Cornish miners in the New World in the Early Nineteenth Century' Cornish Studies, Vol 9, (2001)

Dr S. P. Schwartz, 'Cornish migration studies: An epistomological and paradigmatic critique' Cornish Studies, Vol 10, (2002)

Journals

Transactions of the Royal Geological Society of Cornwall

Transactions of the Royal Institution of Cornwall

Transactions of the Royal Cornwall Polytechnic Society

Newspapers

Royal Cornwall Gazette

West Briton

Mining Journal

Parish Registers

Camborne

Illogan

Redruth

ACKNOWLEDGEMENTS

There are many people who have helped me in the production of this book. The late Donald James first told me of the manuscript's existence and Jay Foote, of the Camborne School of Mines library, gave me access to it. I am grateful to both of them. Professor Charles Thomas has been a constant source of information on the people involved in the book and the background to it. I am also grateful for his Foreword to the book. To other members of the Thomas family I am especially grateful for their permission to reproduce pages from the original manuscript: Monica, Linda, Simon and Leonard Thomas. David Thomas of Camborne, and the staff at the Cornwall Record Office, Terry Knight and the staff at the Cornwall Centre and Angela Broome and the staff at the RCM, have all been extremely helpful in my search for explanations and support for my arguments. To Jack Trounson, Tom Harris and Tom Morrison I am also very grateful, for their extensive writings on the history of Dolcoath Mine, which I have used freely. Sharron Schwartz read and commented on the section on bal maidens, for which I thank her. I must also thank Heather and Ivan Corbett, who have been very helpful and encouraging in bringing this project to a conclusion. My wife, Sonia, as always, has given me constant support and has read my manuscript through at each stage of revision. Many others have offered explanations and thoughts on aspects of this book over the last few years, and if their names have been missed here, I apologise.